The National Trust

GARDENER'S
ALMANAC
2024

The National Trust

GARDENER'S ALMANAC

2024

Greg Loades

National Trust

Published by National Trust Books
An imprint of HarperCollins Publishers
1 London Bridge Street, London SE1 9GF
www.harpercollins.co.uk

HarperCollins Publishers
Macken House, 39/40 Mayor Street Upper, Dublin 1, D01 C9W8, Ireland

First published in 2023

ISBN 978-0-00-856762-0

10 9 8 7 6 5 4 3 2 1

❧ CONTENTS ❧

❧ INTRODUCTION ❧

It's amazing how much our gardens change over the course of a year. Bare patches of ground in May are full to bursting by July. Delicate little courgette seedlings, lovingly nurtured on the windowsill at the beginning of spring, are a force of nature by the end of July, pumping out hefty fruits so rapidly that you'll probably feel like shouting 'Stop!' at them at some point. Likewise, packets of cornflower seeds emptied hopefully onto bare earth in April can be setting seed of their own before summer is out.

Whatever the time of year, a garden never stands still. Even in winter, when frost, fog and cold make summer days seem almost mythical, there will be signs of life. Maybe it's the twittering of a robin, warning off intruders, or the pecking of a fieldfare, venturing into gardens to find berries to survive the winter cold.

While the garden changes through the year, so do gardeners. For me, one of the joys of gardening is the changes of pace that ebb and flow as the calendar ticks by. Sometimes the garden is a place of frenzied sowing, planting, mulching or watering. At others, it is simply a place to 'be' and escape from all the other things that are vying for my attention.

More than ever, I feel that to have a garden is not to have an escape from the real world, but a passport into it. This is the world of living things that pre-dates all the noise of modern life that, at times, can feel suffocating. I always feel better when I'm in the garden.

I hope this book will serve as a useful companion through the year as you discover the delights and wonders of being out in the garden month after month. We all need reminders, and in these pages there are lots of suggestions for what can be done each month to make the garden more fruitful and colourful, as well as wildlife friendly.

If there are some gardening tasks that you've not been able to crack, National Trust gardeners are here to help, explaining how they look after some of the most iconic plants and features from the country's most renowned gardens each month. I find visiting gardens a great source of inspiration when choosing what to grow at home, and some timely advice from the experts will help turn inspiration into reality.

Whatever your plans and schemes for your garden for the coming year, I hope you enjoy every second of being out there, with this guide and a mug of something refreshing close to hand, to help you on your way.

Happy gardening.

Greg Loades

Witch hazel

January

'*Every gardener's New Year starts*
with a euphoric gush of hope.'
– Christopher Lloyd

In the garden, January is not a month for the faint-hearted. Even the keenest gardener might be more inclined to relax indoors with a good book than put their boots on and tackle a bit of pruning. But my goodness, it's worth it if you do. An hour spent gardening in January, when daylight is scarce and signs of life are hard to come by, feels like a bit of a steal. The ground can be too wet to stand on for most of the month, or frozen and unworkable. In short, January is a month to savour the 'little victories'. Enjoy the occasional moments spent in the garden snipping or tidying, the playful movement of a robin, or seeing the first signs of early bulbs if the month turns out to be mild.

Location	Date	Rise	Set
Belfast			
	Jan 01 (Mon)	08:46 GMT	16:08 GMT
	Jan 11 (Thu)	08:41 GMT	16:22 GMT
	Jan 21 (Sun)	08:31 GMT	16:39 GMT
	Jan 31 (Wed)	08:16 GMT	16:59 GMT
Cardiff			
	Jan 01 (Mon)	08:18 GMT	16:14 GMT
	Jan 11 (Thu)	08:15 GMT	16:26 GMT
	Jan 21 (Sun)	08:06 GMT	16:42 GMT
	Jan 31 (Wed)	07:53 GMT	17:00 GMT
Edinburgh			
	Jan 01 (Mon)	08:44 GMT	15:49 GMT
	Jan 11 (Thu)	08:38 GMT	16:03 GMT
	Jan 21 (Sun)	08:26 GMT	16:22 GMT
	Jan 31 (Wed)	08:10 GMT	16:43 GMT
London			
	Jan 01 (Mon)	08:07 GMT	16:02 GMT
	Jan 11 (Thu)	08:04 GMT	16:14 GMT
	Jan 21 (Sun)	07:55 GMT	16:30 GMT
	Jan 31 (Wed)	07:42 GMT	16:47 GMT

❧ WEATHER CHARTS ❧

Averages 1991–2020

Location

Belfast	Max temperature (°C)	8.20
	Min temperature (°C)	2.18
	Days of air frost (days)	7.47
	Sunshine (hours)	40.12
	Rainfall (mm)	88.51
	Days of rainfall ≥1 mm (days)	14.44
Cardiff	Max temperature (°C)	8.58
	Min temperature (°C)	2.5
	Days of air frost (days)	7.8
	Sunshine (hours)	53.53
	Rainfall (mm)	126.97
	Days of rainfall ≥1 mm (days)	15.6
Edinburgh	Max temperature (°C)	7.29
	Min temperature (°C)	1.67
	Days of air frost (days)	9.03
	Sunshine (hours)	55.17
	Rainfall (mm)	64.66
	Days of rainfall ≥1 mm (days)	12.43
London	Max temperature (°C)	7.46
	Min temperature (°C)	2.29
	Days of air frost (days)	7.92
	Sunshine (hours)	60.02
	Rainfall (mm)	69.54
	Days of rainfall ≥1 mm (days)	12.07

❧ TASKS ❧

Things to start

Chillies
Chillies need a long growing season in order to produce a good crop of well-ripened fruits. If you're growing outside, they'll also need a good summer, but you can give them every chance of a hot, bountiful crop by sowing early. Sow chillies on the surface of dampened peat-free compost in an 8cm (3in) pot with a thin layer of sieved compost or vermiculite. Keep in a heated propagator, or in one placed in a well-lit part of the house. If you don't have a propagator, you can put a clear plastic bag over the pot and secure it with an elastic band. If the compost goes dry and dusty, gently water it. Place a saucer under the pot and half fill it with water at room temperature. After five minutes, pour away any standing water. Seeds will take a week or two to germinate. When they do, remove the cover.

Roses
If the soil isn't too wet underfoot it's the perfect time to plant roses, either ones bought in pots or bare-root ones. Roses are hungry plants, so mixing a spadeful of compost, or well-rotted manure, along with a sprinkle of mycorrhizal fungi, into the bottom of each planting hole will help them grow. Whether planting potted or bare-root roses, make sure the bulky part of the rose at the bottom of the stem is buried as this will stop the plant from drying out in hot weather and keep it well anchored. Firm the soil around the plant with the ball of your foot. Water well once, not watering again until spring, unless conditions are very dry.

Things to finish

Leeks
Leeks can look very attractive in winter when left in the soil and enhanced by a hoar frost, especially frost-tolerant varieties such as 'Oarsman'. Lift them with a digging fork as and when you want them, as long as the soil isn't frozen solid. The act of harvesting will help break up large clods of soil and once lifted, leave the bare soil to be broken down by future frosts.

Brussels sprouts
Brussels sprouts are one of the few crops that can actually be 'picked' in winter. They are fresher and tastier if picked straight from the stem just before cooking. You may want to wear gloves in freezing conditions or your hands are likely to go numb. Hold each sprout and push down on it with your thumb. Don't forget, you can also cut off the top of the plant and cook it like you would a cabbage.

❧ SOMETHING TO PRUNE ❧

Climbing roses

When winters are mild, climbing roses could still have
flowers on them. It's still best to cut them back at this point
to shape them up ready for the new growing season. If
growing a rose against a wall, fan out the stems horizontally
to encourage flowering sideshoots and trim back leading
stems that have grown too long. Cut back sideshoots of the
main stems by half and remove stems that are crossing into
others. If growing a climber up a trellis or pillar, trim the
ends of long stems as desired and remove any stems that
can't be trained comfortably to their supports. Along with
pruning, removing all the old foliage is an important job as it
will prevent fungal disease from infecting new shoots.

❧ SOMETHING TO SAVOUR ❧

Laying plans for the future

Take some time to walk around the garden and observe
it in its 'skeleton' form. Rather than lamenting the lack of
warmth and signs of life, survey the scene and think about
the parts of the garden that you like the most and those
you'd like to change. I find it much easier to come up with
ideas for new features, re-siting plants or changing areas
when the garden is 'asleep' and there are fewer jobs on the
gardening to-do list to distract me.

❧ THRIFTY PROJECT ❧

If you think that taking cuttings is too fiddly, or requires special propagation equipment, take some hardwood cuttings this month and you might change your mind. All you need is a pair of secateurs and a little area of bare soil, or a bit of compost, and a few deep pots. Cut healthy, young woody stems of plants such as abelia, dogwoods, gooseberries, currants and buddleja. Shorten them to 30cm (12in) long, making a flat cut at the bottom, just below a bud, and a slanted cut at the top just above a bud. Push them into the soil outside or into deep pots (the ones roses or fruit bushes are sold in will work) filled with soil-based compost, so they are half covered. Mix some grit into the soil outside if it is heavy. Leave them outdoors until the following autumn when you should have rooted plants to move to their new home.

HEAD GARDENER'S JOB
❧ OF THE MONTH ❧

Pruning laburnum at Bodnant Garden, Conwy
Head Gardener – Ned Lomax

Bodnant's famous Laburnum Arch is the oldest and longest in the UK. Devised by Bodnant's owner, Henry Davis Pochin, and planted in 1878, the original plants of *Laburnum anagyriodes* were soon removed and replaced with the *Laburnum* x *watereri* 'Vossii' variety, which produces longer racemes of flowers and fewer seeds.

We train and tie the laburnum plants into an arched framework, which allows the flowers to hang down, creating a tunnel of blossom. Each January, two gardeners start the laborious task of untying, pruning and retying each plant, which takes around six weeks to complete. After severing the previous year's knots, any dead or diseased material is removed, as well as the older branches, leaving young and pliable growth for retraining. Each branch is then carefully and snugly tied back onto the framework. After flowering, the plants produce new growth, which we will tie in in the following year.

The Laburnum Arch typically flowers at the end of May or beginning of June. For three weeks it delights visitors who flock in their thousands to take in the amazing sight and scent. After the spectacle is over, we then return to remove the spent flowers, encouraging the plants to direct their energy into new growth.

❧ PLANTS OF THE MONTH ❧

Cornus alba 'Sibirica'
The colourful bare stems of this species of cornus (white or red-barked dogwood) are the ideal antidote to winter gloom: the straightened 'candy canes' make the garden look fun rather than funereal. The one-year-old stems of 'Sibirica' are as red as a ripe strawberry and are very effective if planted in groups throughout the garden. The key to getting the most vibrant colour is to prune each stem back to 10cm (4in) from ground level at the end of winter each year. New growth is brighter and bolder than the old wood. Grow this plant in a sunny spot in damp soil for the best results. Height: up to 2.5m (8ft).

Molinia 'Heidebraut'
This neat, slender grass wins lots of plaudits in late summer and autumn, when its purple stems and plumes of flower transition

to fiery orange and yellow. But when the colour has drained out of them, their wispy aged flower stems add beautiful texture to the garden and make a foil for lush green shades of euphorbias or evergreen shrubs such as euonymus and pittosporum. They also serve as a wistful reminder of the last golden days of summer in the depths of winter. Height: 1.5m (5ft).

Hamamelis x intermedia 'Jelena'

A witch hazel in full bloom in winter is as mysterious as it is intoxicating. Its wonderful perfume and fiery, spidery strands cut through the pervading cold and low light levels of January. 'Jelena' shows intense, beautiful shades and is best planted in a sheltered, sunny or partly shaded place, in an acid to neutral soil that stays moist, but drains well enough to not get waterlogged easily. The flowers are a food source for pollinating insects. Height: up to 4m (13ft).

❧ WILDLIFE TO LOOK FOR ❧

Hedgehogs

Hedgehogs spend the winter in piles of fallen leaves in sheltered corners, which they will use to make nests. They may also spend the winter underneath garden sheds. Resist the urge to tidy up sheltered corners of the garden until the end of March, to allow them to come out of hibernation first.

Grey squirrels

Though less active in winter than at other times of the year, these energetic rodents can be spotted at bird feeding stations in search of easy nuts. They can harm bird populations by eating eggs though, so it's a good idea to invest in squirrel-proof bird feeders if they are active in your garden. It's near impossible to keep squirrels out of the garden, but cover bulbs

in pots with chicken wire until they start shooting, to deter
squirrels from digging them up.

Early bees

You may see a bumblebee, or maybe even an early mining
bee or two if the weather conditions are sunny and
temperatures regularly hit double figures. Winter flowers
such as mahonia, single-flowered hellebores and *Clematis
cirrhosa* are all useful sources of nectar for them.

❧ HOW TO HELP WILDLIFE ❧

Some of the old seedheads and flower stems left intact on
perennials can start to look tatty or fall over in the garden.
If you tidy them up, leave the pile of old material in a
dry, sheltered corner of the garden to provide a home for
overwintering insects such as ladybirds – they will be valuable
aphid-eaters in spring and summer. If you've pruned thick,
woodier material from shrubs and trees, pile these up in
a shady corner along with any leaves and dead grass that's
been raked off the lawn. This will provide an ideal habitat for
mammals and invertebrates, from hedgehogs to ground beetles.

❧ BIRDS OF THE MONTH ❧

Blue tit

One of the most beautiful garden birds, with its distinctive
lemon-yellow breast and soft blue feathers, the blue tit is a
common winter visitor. Harsh winters can reduce numbers
considerably, but gardens can offer welcome refuge. Blue
tits will seek out nest boxes in winter where they will roost
in groups to keep warm. As the temperature falls, nuts and

seeds in feeding stations are valuable food for them, as are ivy berries and sunflower seeds.

Redwing

This small bird looks very similar to a song thrush at first glance but differs with its trademark orangey-red underwing markings. It also has a creamy-white stripe just above its eye. The smallest thrush in the UK, it is usually a field-dwelling bird, picking off berries from surrounding hedgerows. It may venture into gardens on very cold days or when the ground is covered in snow, especially if there are windfall apples on the ground.

❧ GARDEN EVENTS ❧

Houseplant Week, 8–14 January

January is a great month for appreciating houseplants. Treat yourself to a new one to lift the mood indoors and keep you in touch with growing things.

Squirrel Appreciation Day, 21 January

You might think twice about joining in with this day, as squirrels can be a bit of a nuisance for gardeners. Watching squirrels can be great fun though, especially if you have children. Go and spot them at your local park, rather than in the garden.

RSPB Big Garden Birdwatch, 26–28 January

It's time to spend an hour watching the birds that visit your garden and record the results for the RSPB. The surveys submitted allow the RSPB to obtain a picture of what bird species are in decline throughout the UK and how to best help them.

NATIONAL TRUST GARDENS
❧ AT THEIR BEST ❧
(for winter walks)

Anglesey Abbey, Cambridgeshire

With over a hundred acres of winter garden, Anglesey Abbey makes for a magnificent walk on a frosty morning. Follow the winding paths as an array of winter colours, textures and perfumes in packed borders entertain you along the way.

Trivia
The gardens at Anglesey Abbey, Cambridgeshire, are home to four ranks of horse chestnut trees, some over 400 metres tall and planted in 1937 for the coronation of King George VI.

Mottisfont, Hampshire

An acre of winter garden will delight and brighten up the dullest of days, with an exciting collection of berries, stems and early bulbs. Ground cover vincas and pachysandra are planted in 'streams' while dogwoods and brambles show off their bright winter stems.

The Argory, Co. Armagh

Winter is a good time to spot wildlife on a woodland walk at The Argory, with foraging robins at your feet and the chance to see perching kingfishers above the River Blackwater. Towards the end of winter, snowdrops will bring further seasonal cheer.

Trivia
The Vyne, Hampshire, harbours an English oak (Quercus robur) which is about 500 years old. It is completely hollow inside and supported by two metal props.

Dunham Massey, Cheshire

Enjoy a massive seven acres of winter garden, with striking white-stemmed birches lighting up the landscape, underplanted with snowdrops. Designed with the help of legendary plantsman Roy Lancaster, there are more than 1,600 winter shrubs, trees and evergreens to enjoy and be inspired by.

Bodnant Garden, Conwy

The famous winter garden trail at Bodnant will take you through 250 years of garden history and is full of planting ideas for adding bright and bold winter features to your own garden. Dogwoods, heathers, bergenias and conifers make this a garden that can rival summer with its range of colours.

'Once inside this great garden, in which every device of every good school of English gardening has been used, you are inside the English gardener's dream.'
– Edward Hyams on Bodnant Garden

YOUR NOTES FOR
✎ NEXT YEAR ✎

What has worked

What hasn't

What I'd like to try

Snowdrops

February

'There is always in February,
some one day, at least, when one smells
the yet distant but surely coming, summer.'
– Gertrude Jekyll

February gives with one hand and takes away with the other. On mild, sunny days, it can feel like mid-spring for an hour or two, until darkness falls at 5.30pm to put excited gardeners back in their place. There is, however, an overriding feeling of momentum building in the garden, as the daylight hours get noticeably longer and colourful signs of growth begin to appear. Early iris, crocus, winter aconites and snowdrops start to flower, while the emerging tips of foliage from spring's brasher, more 'heavyweight' bulbs, such as large-flowered daffodils, are a tantalising foretaste of the spring joy to come.

❧ SUNRISE AND SUNSET 2024 ❧

Location	Date	Rise	Set
Belfast			
	Feb 01 (Thu)	08:14 GMT	17:01 GMT
	Feb 11 (Sun)	07:55 GMT	17:22 GMT
	Feb 21 (Wed)	07:53 GMT	17:43 GMT
	Feb 29 (Thu)	07:14 GMT	17:59 GMT
Cardiff			
	Feb 01 (Thu)	07:52 GMT	17:01 GMT
	Feb 11 (Sun)	07:35 GMT	17:20 GMT
	Feb 21 (Wed)	07:16 GMT	17:38 GMT
	Feb 29 (Thu)	06:59 GMT	17:52 GMT
Edinburgh			
	Feb 01 (Thu)	08:08 GMT	16:45 GMT
	Feb 11 (Sun)	07:48 GMT	17:07 GMT
	Feb 21 (Wed)	07:25 GMT	17:29 GMT
	Feb 29 (Thu)	07:05 GMT	17:46 GMT
London			
	Feb 01 (Thu)	07:40 GMT	16:49 GMT
	Feb 11 (Sun)	07:24 GMT	17:07 GMT
	Feb 21 (Wed)	07:04 GMT	17:26 GMT
	Feb 29 (Thu)	06:48 GMT	17:40 GMT

❧ WEATHER CHARTS ❧

Averages 1991–2020

Location

Belfast	Max temperature (°C)	8.78
	Min temperature (°C)	2.13
	Days of air frost (days)	6.75
	Sunshine (hours)	65.16
	Rainfall (mm)	70.26
	Days of rainfall ≥1 mm (days)	12.65
Cardiff	Max temperature (°C)	9.15
	Min temperature (°C)	2.47
	Days of air frost (days)	7.27
	Sunshine (hours)	76.15
	Rainfall (mm)	92.97
	Days of rainfall ≥1 mm (days)	12.00
Edinburgh	Max temperature (°C)	7.96
	Min temperature (°C)	1.72
	Days of air frost (days)	8.84
	Sunshine (hours)	82.23
	Rainfall (mm)	53.05
	Days of rainfall ≥1 mm (days)	9.83
London	Max temperature (°C)	8.07
	Min temperature (°C)	2.25
	Days of air frost (days)	7.48
	Sunshine (hours)	76.06
	Rainfall (mm)	51.41
	Days of rainfall ≥1 mm (days)	10.65

❧ TASKS ❧

Things to start

F

Early potatoes

Although potato planting begins in earnest towards the end of March (weather permitting), February is the ideal time to begin helping them to sprout (also known as chitting). It's not the end of the world if you don't get around to doing it, but there's something exciting about handling the tubers that will result in delicious, flavour-filled new potatoes in early summer. Start with varieties labelled as 'first earlies'. These are traditionally the varieties that are harvested in early summer as new potatoes and include favourites such as the waxy 'Pentland Javelin' and high yielding 'Rocket'. To prepare them for planting, position each tuber with the end that holds the cluster of 'eyes' facing up – egg boxes or cell trays are ideal for this. Keep them in a well-lit, cool room indoors until the tubers have short, fat shoots around 2cm (¾in) long. It will take at least a month until the tubers are ready for planting, once soil conditions are dry underfoot.

Snowdrops

Snowdrop experts will tell you that the best way to plant snowdrops is as dry bulbs in the summer – but it's a fiendish job to remember where they are, or where you may want more snowdrops, when the garden is bursting at the seams in the summer months and late-winter bulbs are perhaps not at the forefront of our minds. If you want to add more of these bulbs – or split up thick, broad clumps into smaller ones, to spread around the garden and make rows or drifts of flowers – you can do it as the flowers fade and the plants are still in leaf. Prepare the holes where you want to put new plants.

Then, loosen the soil and add a good handful of leaf mould or well-rotted home-made compost, mixing it into the hole thoroughly. Choose a planting site that is in partial shade, avoiding very dry soil, beneath large trees.

To lift and divide your snowdrops:

1. Insert a spade or digging fork vertically into the soil around 10cm (4in) from the edge of the clump, loosening the soil all around it.

2. Lift up your spade or fork to uproot the clump of snowdrops. Separate the clump into new sections, making sure each one contains at least four bulbs.

3. Plant immediately into the prepared holes, planting at the same depth as before, then water well.

Things to finish

Parsnips

This Christmas dinner staple deserves to be far more than a festive novelty. Parsnips can be an almost ever-present crop on the veg patch, with the last roots harvested in February, before sowing begins again in March. However many you have left to dig up, clear the surplus this month to make space for fresh crops that need starting in early spring. Insert a digging fork all the way along the rows to loosen the soil and carefully lift the ground to see what treasure lies beneath. All the foliage is likely to have died back by now, so you may be pleasantly surprised to find more roots than you realise. They will keep for a few weeks in an unheated shed or garage and are delicious in soup or stew.

Cabbages

Hearty, healthy – and unfairly blighted by the miserable school dinners of yesteryear – cabbages are always in season. It's time to cut the last of the winter crop that have been sitting like statues through the colder months, before the weather starts to warm up and they begin to lose their freshness. This will also help free up more space in the garden. Cabbages do a good job of breaking up soil, making potatoes the ideal replacement crop, easily planted into the already loosened soil.

❧ SOMETHING TO PRUNE ❦

Group 3 clematis

Late-flowering clematis (also known as Group 3 clematis) are the ones that start to bloom from late June onwards. They are by far the simplest type of clematis to grow as they flower on growth made in the current growing season, making pruning a quick and uncomplicated task and providing great results. Towards the end of the month, cut all the stems back to 10cm (4in) from ground level, making a cut just above a fat growth bud. After you've cleared away all the old growth, pull up any weeds and remove any snails that were hiding beneath the top growth. Spread a mulch of well-rotted compost 5cm (2in) thick around the base of the plant, making sure not to touch any of the new growth. Watch as new growth emerges and flowers form within the year.

❧ SOMETHING TO SAVOUR ❧

Carpets of tiny bulbs

The flowers of tiny, early spring bulbs such as snowdrops, winter aconites, *Iris reticulata* 'Katharine Hodgkin' and *Crocus tommasinianus* are the children's birthday presents of the garden: loved and adored when eyes are first set on them, enjoyed for a few weeks, then forgotten until a new set come along in a year's time. Savour the excitement of these intricate flowers lighting up wet, soggy, monochrome landscapes. A handful of cut blooms will bring a flourish to any kitchen windowsill when the gloom of a long winter is beginning to take its toll. Early bulbs speak of hope, resilience and better days to come. Their virtues are a tonic for life, not just for February.

Lighter evenings

At some point in February – probably in the second half of the month, on a cloudless day – there's a good chance that you'll experience that moment when an afternoon pottering about in the garden lasts noticeably longer than it has for a while. As the sun sets and you take a minute to stand still and look at the garden, there's a feeling of everything moving in the right direction – of warmer, lighter evenings to come, of nature having recharged its batteries and being ready to do it all over again.

⊰ THRIFTY PROJECT ⊱

Sorting through seeds

Coat pockets, shelves under sinks, tables by the back door and random cupboards – that's where I tend to find lots of gardening gold dust, otherwise known as leftover packets of seeds. Gathering all your old seed packets together is a great job this month. See what you've got to hand (I tend to throw away any packets from the year before last, unless I can directly sow them outside) and work out what gaps you have. Aside from saving you money, gathering all the packets together in one place also presents the perfect opportunity to organise them by what needs sowing when. You can even set reminders on your phone. A message to 'sow carrots' might be the perfect excuse to avoid something you would rather not be doing.

HEAD GARDENER'S JOB
❧ OF THE MONTH ❧

Hazel coppicing at Dyffryn Gardens, Vale of Glamorgan
Head Gardener – Chris Flynn

At Dyffryn, we harvest hazel from across the garden for 'pea sticks' and bean poles, which make great plant supports. By cutting down hazel on a rotation (in our case, every seven to eight years) you promote lots of new, heavily branched growth, which is perfect for weaving together to hold up perennials throughout the year.

1. From December to February, using a hand saw, we cut down all the stems growing from the hazel stool to 30cm (12in) above ground level.

2. Next, we remove all the heavily branched 'brash' material. It should be no thicker than thumb width and in as long a piece as possible for weaving.

3. We then separate out long, straight stems for beanpoles and cut down wrist-thick sections into 30cm (12in) logs – these can be dried for firewood or used to make charcoal.

4. Finally, we tie up the brash or pea sticks into bundles to make them easier to transport and pile small material to encourage wildlife.

We'll use the pea sticks to make baskets to support herbaceous perennials, stopping them from flopping onto other plants, as well as supporting the seed heads through winter for foraging birds and sheltering insects. The seven-to-eight year rotation provides a habitat for dormice, which use the plant as a food source and arboreal transport system.

❧ PLANTS OF THE MONTH ❧

Galanthus 'S. Arnott'
Compared to many garden plants, snowdrops are delicate and dainty little numbers – hope in miniature. Some are bolder than others though, and 'S. Arnott' is the big-boned cousin of the common snowdrop *Galanthus nivalis*. It stands noticeably taller (up to 30cm in height) and the flowers are much larger, with a green v-shaped marking in the centre and a honey scent. If the common snowdrop is looking a bit 'lost' in your garden, 'S. Arnott' is a more noticeable alternative. Height: 30cm (12in).

Crocus chrysanthus 'Cream Beauty'
One of February's tiniest plants has the ability to create both a stunning and compact display of winter beauty. 'Cream Beauty' is very effective at adding a pop of colour, crammed into a container of gritty compost on a small patio, or lighting up large lawns or grassy areas under trees. It thrives in free-draining soil in sun or semi-shade. Each corm can carry three to four beautiful scented blooms, with cream petals, deepening to buttercup yellow in the centre. Height: 8cm (3in).

Daphne bholua 'Jacqueline Postill'
If you're already tired of the perfume you were bought for Christmas, breathe in the aroma of this sweetly scented flowering shrub in February. Hardy down to -10°C (14°F), it can be grown in a well-drained sheltered spot with morning

sun and shade in the afternoon. It is evergreen in all but the coldest weather and is a useful nectar source for early bumblebees. You may even spot the red admiral butterfly enjoying it on very mild days this month. Height: 2m (6.6ft).

❧ WILDLIFE TO LOOK FOR ❧

Rabbits

Rabbits are always on the lookout for food from the garden and this month they are likely to make bark, bulb shoots and grass their priorities. Use closely meshed wire netting to protect bulbs and place guards around young trees, which can be severely damaged by a hungry rabbit.

Frogs and toads

The warm environment of the compost heap can be a key hibernating spot for frogs and toads. In milder parts of the country, you may start to see frog and toadspawn in ponds towards the end of the month. Frogspawn is laid in clumps and toadspawn in chains over submerged plants.

Foxes

Foxes are active all year round and could be attracted to your garden in the winter months when searching for food. It is very difficult to keep foxes out of a garden using barriers, but if there is no easy access to food then they are less likely to cause a problem. Avoid using strong-smelling plant food such as bonemeal or chicken manure pellets, which is likely to attract them.

❧ HOW TO HELP WILDLIFE ❧

Clear away any snow and ice to give birds a helping hand this month, providing them with easier access to food and water. Melt ice in bird baths with warm water, and clear small areas in snow-covered lawns to give birds the chance to forage for insects. Create paths to bird feeding stations by sprinkling salt or scraping away snow with a shovel, so you can keep feeders topped up at the most crucial time of the year.

❧ BIRDS OF THE MONTH ❧

Mistle thrush
Towards the end of the month, these early nesters begin to build their untidy, cup-shaped nests, often in the fork of a tree. They work as a team, with both parents looking after the chicks. Their ideal territory includes large trees and short grass, so you're most likely to find them in bigger gardens. Mistle thrushes may have a second brood later in the year.

Great spotted woodpecker
What's that drumming sound? Probably from the industrious work of the great spotted woodpecker. Males are able to drum at tree trunks 20 times a second, to ward off competition for territory. A beautiful bird, it has black-and-white spotted wings and a red head and rump. Males have a scarlet patch on the back of their heads. Solid trees are required for drumming but they prefer to peck at softer, rotting wood when searching for food such as insects.

❧ GARDEN EVENTS ❧

National Nest Box Week, 14–21 February

This week puts breeding birds in the spotlight and encourages everyone to put up a nest box or two in their garden. A nest box in a sheltered site is ideal, placed at least 1m (3ft) above ground level.

Snowdrop season

February is snowdrop season and many National Trust gardens open their gates to show off their inspiring snowdrop collections (see page 41). While the common snowdrop (*Galanthus nivalis*) is a familiar garden plant, there are hundreds of rare and unusual cultivated varieties that are highly collectible; a single bulb of a choice form can change hands for hundreds of pounds among snowdrop enthusiasts, known as galanthophiles. In 2022, a single bulb of *Galanthus plicatus* 'Golden Tears' was sold on eBay for £1,850. During February half term, Wallington, Northumberland, holds snowdrop planting sessions with their gardeners, where they aim to plant 100,000 snowdrops every year.

Cleveden Spring Trail

Start to look out for the earliest signs of spring in February half term on the Cleveden, Buckinghamshire, spring trail as you journey through the glorious gardens and woodland overlooking the River Thames.

Brilliant Birds Trail

Take a journey to Arlington Court, Devon, and take part in a free tour to discover some of the brilliant birds that call the estate home.

Camellia season
The whole month is a celebration of these glorious late winter flowers at Chiswick House, where their conservatory can be enjoyed in full bloom – one of the oldest collections under glass in Europe.

Seed swaps
Early February is a good time to get the seed sowing year underway, with many summer flowers best sown soon, and a seed swap event can help boost your plant stocks without having to spend a lot of money. Check gardenorganic.org for a seed swap event near you.

Kew Orchid Festival
Kew's famous festival runs throughout the month, with sensational glasshouse displays of orchids from around the world. It's a great pick-me-up if you find yourself in the capital on a cold winter's day.

'Lone flower, hemmed in with
snows and white as they.'
– William Wordsworth, 'To a Snowdrop'

NATIONAL TRUST GARDENS
❧ AT THEIR BEST ❧
(for snowdrops)

Chirk Castle, Wrexham
Snowdrops are planted all around this famous garden, among clipped yews, herbaceous borders, shrubs and rock gardens, but the best displays are in the Pleasure Ground Wood, next to the Formal Garden.

Oxburgh Hall, Norfolk
Thousands of snowdrops and winter aconites put on a memorable display each year in the Wilderness, My Lady's Wood and on the North Terrace. The plants are allowed to self-seed, creating a beautiful, natural scene.

Trivia
England's largest wood of Arbutus unedo (strawberry tree) lies along a steep bank on the south side of Dunster Castle. Over 400 trees were planted there by the Trust between 1978 and 1981.

Fountains Abbey and Studley Royal Water Garden, North Yorkshire
The spectacular drifts of snowdrops at this World Heritage Site are a legacy of Earl de Grey, who planted the flowers along the banks of the River Skell when he owned the estate during the nineteenth century.

Polesden Lacey, Surrey
Snowdrops can be found mingling with winter aconites in the colourful and richly scented winter garden, inspired by the life of renowned horticulturist Graham Stuart Thomas. They are also planted in the Lime Walk.

Dunster Castle, Somerset

The 28 acres of parkland around Dunster Castle is the perfect setting for an idyllic winter walk, with patches of snowdrops dotted all around the area, as well as growing in the garden borders.

Trivia
A yew tree at Shugborough, Staffordshire, has a crown circumference (the spread of its branches) of a staggering 175m (575ft), the widest of any tree in the UK.

'A garden revealed all at once is like a story told before it is started.'
– Dan Pearson

YOUR NOTES FOR
❧ NEXT YEAR ❧

What has worked

_____

_____

_____

_____

_____

_____

What hasn't

_____

_____

_____

_____

What I'd like to try

_____

_____

_____

_____

_____

_____

_____

Onions

March

'*The more one gardens, the more one learns;
and the more one learns, the more one
realizes how little one knows.*'
–Vita Sackville-West

March is often the most unpredictable month in the garden. It can be a time of freshly mown grass, daffodils in full bloom and sowing vegetables outdoors. But it can also see frost and snow, as if the arrival of spring is on hold – 'buffering' rather than bursting into life. Whatever the weather, change is in the air. Evenings are getting lighter, buds are beginning to fatten on bare branches, and the earliest perennials are pushing their young shoots above the soil. By the end of the month, there's a feeling of relief. Even if it's cold outside, the growing season is beginning again, and momentum is building.

❧ SUNRISE AND SUNSET 2024 ❧

Location	Date	Rise	Set
Belfast			
	Mar 01 (Fri)	07:12 GMT	18:01 GMT
	Mar 11 (Mon)	06:48 GMT	18:21 GMT
	Mar 21 (Thu)	06:23 GMT	18:40 GMT
	Mar 31 (Sun)	07:57 GMT	19:59 GMT
Cardiff			
	Mar 01 (Fri)	06:57 GMT	17:54 GMT
	Mar 11 (Mon)	06:35 GMT	18:11 GMT
	Mar 21 (Thu)	06:12 GMT	18:28 GMT
	Mar 31 (Sun)	06:49 GMT	19:45 GMT
Edinburgh			
	Mar 01 (Fri)	07:03 GMT	17:48 GMT
	Mar 11 (Mon)	06:37 GMT	18:09 GMT
	Mar 21 (Thu)	06:11 GMT	18:29 GMT
	Mar 31 (Sun)	06:45 GMT	19:50 GMT
London			
	Mar 01 (Fri)	06:45 GMT	17:42 GMT
	Mar 11 (Mon)	06:23 GMT	17:59 GMT
	Mar 21 (Thu)	06:00 GMT	18:16 GMT
	Mar 31 (Sun)	06:38 GMT	19:33 GMT

❧ WEATHER CHARTS ❧

Averages 1991–2020

Location		
Belfast	Max temperature (°C)	10.48
	Min temperature (°C)	3.12
	Days of air frost (days)	4.39
	Sunshine (hours)	97.71
	Rainfall (mm)	71.37
	Days of rainfall ≥1 mm (days)	12.64
Cardiff	Max temperature (°C)	11.31
	Min temperature (°C)	3.91
	Days of air frost (days)	3.93
	Sunshine (hours)	116.59
	Rainfall (mm)	85.29
	Days of rainfall ≥1 mm (days)	12.29
Edinburgh	Max temperature (°C)	9.71
	Min temperature (°C)	2.93
	Days of air frost (days)	5.77
	Sunshine (hours)	117.32
	Rainfall (mm)	48.48
	Days of rainfall ≥1 mm (days)	9.83
London	Max temperature (°C)	10.91
	Min temperature (°C)	3.72
	Days of air frost (days)	3.69
	Sunshine (hours)	114.20
	Rainfall (mm)	42.82
	Days of rainfall ≥1 mm (days)	9.06

❧ TASKS ❧

Things to start

Onions and shallots

Planting onion and shallot bulbs is one of my favourite gardening jobs to do with my children – there's so little that can go wrong. For a four-year-old, pushing the little bulbs into the soil and covering them up seems a wondrous and exciting thing, and so it should be for all of us. Choose a sunny patch with well-draining soil. In heavy clay soil, the bulbs can rot, and in March it can be a long wait before the soil dries out sufficiently for planting to be done without making a muddy mess. Push the bulbs into the soil with the flat end at the bottom, spacing them 15cm (6in) apart and the rows 30cm (12in) apart. You can space them a bit closer if you want to harvest some of the bulbs as spring onions in early summer. Harvest them in intervals to leave space for the other onions to mature.

Lilies

The window of opportunity for planting these spectacular summer flowers is wide. Planting a couple of potfulls in January, February and March is a small investment of time and will result in a succession of summer blooms that suggests far more work than the effort involved. The key to success with lilies is good drainage. Plant them in deep pots of half and half multi-purpose and soil-based compost and mix a good handful of grit into each pot. Plant the bulbs at three times their depth, leaving a 5cm (2in) gap around the bulbs in each direction. Cover the soil with a grit layer once planting is finished. Place the pots in the sunniest position possible, but ideally with shelter from strong winds.

Things to finish

Forced rhubarb
Clumps of rhubarb that were covered with pots, buckets
– or maybe even a posh terracotta rhubarb forcer – will
be ready to harvest this month. Sweet, succulent stems of
forced rhubarb are a delicacy that has to be tried if you've
only eaten unforced stems. The feeling of pulling these fresh
stems and turning them into a hot pudding straight from the
garden is a special one. It's hard not to feel smug as you tuck
into a hearty helping of forced rhubarb crumble in March.
To harvest the stems, just give them a sharp pull to detach
them at the base. The pale base of the stem is especially sweet
and delicious. Give the clump a rest from harvesting for
the rest of the year, then carry on pulling as normal in the
following spring.

Chard
If chard were a person, they would make you green with
envy. How can it look so perky and beautiful all through
the winter months, even on the darkest, wettest days? Yet
dazzle it does, especially in a biting frost. It's best to harvest
whatever is left this month, to free up more space on your
plot. However, if you have the space, a fresh batch can be
sown again in March, to fill the garden with colour, as
well as providing a regular supply of thick fresh stems and
leaves for many months. 'Fordhook Giant' is a reliable dark
green form with a central white rib, making a good winter
substitute for spinach. For something to make the veg
patch more colourful, grow 'Bright Lights', which has very
attractive stems in orange, bright red and hot pink, to add
some winter cheer. Harvesting a couple of 'Bright Lights'
plants when very small as 'baby leaves' will also add some
wonderful colour to a salad.

❧ SOMETHING TO PRUNE ❧

Winter jasmine

The custard-yellow flowers of winter jasmine (*Jasminum nudiflorum*) are such a welcome sight on cold, dark days, but can easily be forgotten once the flowers fade. Yet this is the time to take steps to make next winter's display better than ever by giving it a timely trim. Despite the graceful blooms, it's a bit of an untidy scrambler, so snip back stems that have just finished flowering, cutting them just above a sideshoot lower down on the plant. Completely snip out a few stems where you've got a bunch of them all growing together, to give those that remain a bit more space. Prune now so that the new growth that forms in spring can carry flowers next winter.

❧ SOMETHING TO SAVOUR ❧

The smell of freshly mown grass

If March starts off mild and dry, it creates the perfect opportunity for an activity that is something of a rite of passage each year. Mowing the lawn for the first time is an activity that transports the gardener from winter into spring, as the smell of freshly mown grass fills the air. The first cut of the year provokes a sort of reflex action: inviting me to rip open seed packets, prepare soil for vegetables, or buy new plants for the border. Such is the power of a familiar fragrance in the garden.

Camellia

A mature camellia in full bloom is sure to lift the spirits this month, and there's something of summer about its showy display. Bright, sometimes blousy flowers set off by glossy green foliage are a real antidote to the still largely bare and twiggy landscape of March. A large camellia in full bloom is the result of many years of establishment, not something that is easily created instantly or bought 'off the shelf'. That's why one in full flower is something to stop and admire.

❧ THRIFTY PROJECT ❧

Sow hardy annuals to make a flower border

Filling an empty border with flowers in one growing season doesn't have to be a costly or difficult task. Hardy annuals are your friends in transforming a bare plot into a full and colourful one. If you've got a patch of garden that isn't ready for permanent plants yet, or that you're undecided about, scatter hardy annuals over it in March. You'll have something beautiful to enjoy this year until you're ready for longer-term plans.

Hardy annuals are also invaluable for filling gaps in between other plants to make borders look fuller. Many of them are small plants, so concentrating them in border edges will work well. Try pot marigolds (*Calendula*) for bright shades of yellow and orange, nigella 'love-in-a-mist' *(Nigella damascena)* for soft blues and pinks and feathery foliage, or bright-red ladybird poppies (*Papaver commutatum*) if you want a 'wildflower' feel. Sow direct onto the surface of light, well-drained soil in a sunny spot in the garden, then gently rake them in.

HEAD GARDENER'S JOB
❧ OF THE MONTH ❧

**Pruning dogwood at Anglesey Abbey, Cambridgeshire
Head Gardener – Kevin Tookey**

M

The winter garden at Anglesey Abbey is home to a collection of plants that are at their best in winter: some for their fragrance, others for their stunning winter stems. Every one to two years, some of these plants are coppiced, pollarded or have old wood removed in spring to produce vibrant stems for the following winter. This is because one- or two-year-old stems are more colourful than older ones.

We have a few species and varieties of dogwood in the winter garden, but the majority are *Cornus alba* and *Cornus sanguinea*. The *Cornus alba* are coppiced annually in spring and *Cornus sanguinea* have three-year-old wood removed because they regenerate very slowly from a hard coppice. We use secateurs and pruning saws to coppice the *Cornus alba* just above ground level and to remove the older wood from the *Cornus sangiunea*. Once they have been pruned, we mulch with well-rotted compost and give the plants a feed with an organic fertiliser using chicken manure pellets.

Dogwoods don't like to dry out in summer, so mulching helps to retain moisture, ameliorate the soil and keep the plant healthy. The chicken manure pellets break down slowly and give the plant extra nutrients to boost their vigour and colour over winter.

❧ PLANTS OF THE MONTH ❧

Pulmonaria 'Trevi Fountain'

It's hard not to have a soft spot for this unassuming perennial.
It's a delight from the moment its leaves – silvery, slender,
spear-shaped and spotted – start to sprout from the ground
this month, while so many herbaceous plants are still asleep.
Next comes the fountain display: masses of blue funnel-
shaped flowers arrange in clusters, much to the delight of
early foraging bees. And it's still a stand-out plant in summer,
when the mature leaves add marvellous texture to the edges
of paths and borders. It grows best in semi-shade.
Height: 30cm (12in).

Bergenia 'Bressingham Ruby'

By the time March arrives, this fine perennial has already
been adding intense colour to the garden for months. Its

large, paddle-shaped leaves show off beautiful shades of burgundy, with crimson undersides a real picture when edged with winter frost. A sure sign that the colder months are behind us can be seen when the foliage colour dulls and tall flower stems rise up, carrying cheerful sprays of bell-shaped, hot-pink flowers. Grow in sun or semi-shade in any soil except those that are very dry or wet. Height: 60cm (2ft).

Magnolia stellata

One of the most magnificent trees for small gardens, this long-flowering magnolia makes the arrival of spring that extra bit special in the garden. Underplanted with crocus or daffodil, it can form the epicentre of a garden with its numerous silky white, sometimes pink-flushed petals, creating a beautiful, flower-filled scene. Naturally spreading outward, you can leave it unpruned to form a multi-stemmed shrub, or remove some of the lower branches in summer to 'lift' the crown and grow it as more of a 'traditional' tree. Grow in a sheltered spot in sun or semi-shade in soil that drains well. Height: 2.5m (8ft).

Viburnum tinus 'Ladybird'

This neat, perky evergreen shrub gives a lot at this time of year in an understated way. Naturally forming a tidy, evergreen mound, it bears hundreds of scented white flowers in clusters, which mingle with pinky red flower buds that are yet to open. This is a good choice if you've seen enormous specimens of *Viburnum tinus* that have been allowed to grow into monstrous light-blocking shrubs, because it is shorter, growing to around 1.5m (5ft) tall. It will grow well in clay or free-draining soil and is best in a sheltered position, although it should be hardy down to -10°C (14°F). Height: 1.5m (5ft).

❧ WILDLIFE TO LOOK FOR ❧

Queen wasps

If the end of winter is mild, queen wasps – slightly larger in size than worker wasps – will start to emerge this month, looking for a suitable place to make a nest. So long as they are not nesting in your roof, try and see wasps not as pests but as valuable pollinators and aphid eaters – an important part of the biodiversity of the garden.

Brimstone butterfly

The pale-yellow brimstone is a herald of spring. Seeing one fluttering around this month is a reminder that warmer days are coming. The males are lemon yellow, while the females are a greenish-white with orange spots in the middle of each wing. Native primroses (*Primula vulgaris*) and dandelions are important early sources of nectar for them this month.

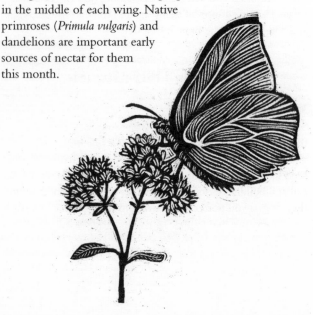

Hares

If your garden backs onto fields then you may well see 'mad' March hares boxing. These entertaining bouts of pugilism are not acts of male bravado, but rather a female telling a male to go away. The brown hare is the most common species you are likely to see on large, flat areas of grassland. Rural areas of East Anglia are hare hotspots.

❧ HOW TO HELP WILDLIFE ❦

Leave out a supply of nesting material to give robins and sparrows a helping hand at building a home. Find a sturdy, multi-branched twig and place dry materials such as straw, seedheads and dry grass in between the branches. Wind soft string around it and add more layers until you've got a ball shape. Then tie a loop of string around the end of the twig and hang it from the branch of a tree.

❧ BIRD OF THE MONTH ❦

Song thrush

Smashed snails on concrete are a giveaway sign that song thrushes are in the garden (unless you also have small children). These neatly spotted songbirds are mainly ground-level feeders and will also be extracting earthworms from the soil and building nests this month. Enjoy the cheerful songs they sing as you potter about in the garden.

✿ GARDEN EVENTS ✿

World Book Day, 7 March
Celebrate World Book Day by visiting one of the National
Trust's second-hand bookshops. The National Trust has more
than 200 shops selling quality second-hand books, including
gardening books, all raising money for the places in their care.

Mothering Sunday, 10 March
Lots of the National Trust's properties will be open for a
family day out. Pay a visit to Nymans, West Sussex, for a
Mother's Day afternoon tea full of home-made treats and
accompanied by live music and glorious views of the Weald.

Easter Trails
A National Trust garden is the place to be for an Easter
adventure. Complete the trail through Dyffryn Gardens,
Vale of Glamorgan, and be rewarded with an Easter treat
or discover some weird and wonderful egg-laying creatures
as you explore the gardens of Scotney Castle, Kent. For the
sporty types, head to Stowe, Buckinghamshire, to take part in
an Easter trail full of sports and games. Most National Trust
Easter events run for the duration of the school holidays,
lasting into April.

Daffodil Festival
Enjoy the annual Daffodil Festival at Cotehele, Cornwall,
as their magnificent collection of more than 300 different
varieties of daffodil, some dating back to the seventeenth
century, show off their cheery blooms.

NATIONAL TRUST GARDENS
❧ AT THEIR BEST ❦
(for daffodils)

Felbrigg Hall, Norfolk
Masses of golden daffodils carpet the lawn in front of the hall at Felbrigg to mark your arrival before you explore the walled garden and 380 acres of landmark trees in the Great Wood.

M

Coughton Court, Warwickshire
The spring garden at Coughton is bursting with thousands of daffodils. It was opened in honour of the late Dr Tom D. Throckmorton, known as the 'Dean of Daffodils', who bred more than 50 different daffodil varieties in his lifetime.

Trivia
The National Collection of rhubarb at Clumber Park consists of more than 130 different varieties of rhubarb, the second largest collection in the world.

Springhill, Londonderry
Welcome in the spring with the magnificent daffodil displays at Springhill, accompanied by some special magnolias and beautiful, white-stemmed birches. The daffodil collection in the walled garden is expanding year by year, with 600 new bulbs added each autumn.

Dunham Massey, Cheshire

There are more than 70 varieties of daffodil to enjoy, including dainty dwarf daffodil 'Tête-à-Tête' in the winter garden, following on from a spectacular display of 50,000 dwarf irises beneath large oak trees.

Powis Castle, Powys

Revel in the dramatic views across the Severn Valley at Powis Castle as spring arrives, with the Daffodil Paddock lit up by thousands of blooms of *Narcissus pseudonarcissus*. Also enjoy violets, magnolias and grape hyacinths at the beginning of spring.

Trivia
The largest rockery in the National Trust is at Sizergh Castle, Cumbria, spanning two thirds of an acre.

'It was one of those March days when the sun shines hot and the wind blows cold: when it is summer in the light, and winter in the shade.'
– Charles Dickens, *Great Expectations*

YOUR NOTES FOR
❧ NEXT YEAR ❧

What has worked

_____

_____

_____

_____

_____

What hasn't

_____

_____

_____

_____

_____

What I'd like to try

_____

_____

_____

_____

_____

_____

_____

_____

Red mason bee on a wallflower

April

'Orchids require patience. Plant them and
then go and concentrate on other things for a
few years and let them surprise you.'
– Jinny Blom

Later in the year, we will look back on April and realise how tidy the garden looked. Many plants and seedlings are in their infancy, and yet it all goes unnoticed amid the excitement of the new growing season. That anything has emerged and is growing at all is enough to give the gardener hope. It is a month of new beginnings. Everything is bursting into life, and there's a lot to undertake, with salads, root crops, potatoes, tomatoes, annual flowers and young perennials all begging to be added to the garden. It is the right time for so much and nature obliges, as daylight lengthens and nights gradually warm up. Buckle up and enjoy the ride.

❧ SUNRISE AND SUNSET 2024 ❧

Location	Date	Rise	Set
Belfast			
	Apr 01 (Mon)	06:55 BST	20:01 BST
	Apr 11 (Thu)	06:30 BST	20:20 BST
	Apr 21 (Sun)	06:06 BST	20:40 BST
	Apr 30 (Tue)	05:46 BST	20:57 BST
Cardiff			
	Apr 01 (Mon)	06:47 BST	19:47 BST
	Apr 11 (Thu)	06:25 BST	20:03 BST
	Apr 21 (Sun)	06:04 BST	20:20 BST
	Apr 30 (Tue)	05:46 BST	20:35 BST
Edinburgh			
	Apr 01 (Mon)	06:42 BST	19:52 BST
	Apr 11 (Thu)	06:16 BST	20:12 BST
	Apr 21 (Sun)	05:52 BST	20:32 BST
	Apr 30 (Tue)	05:30 BST	20:51 BST
London			
	Apr 01 (Mon)	06:35 BST	19:35 BST
	Apr 11 (Thu)	06:13 BST	19:52 BST
	Apr 21 (Sun)	05:52 BST	20:09 BST
	Apr 30 (Tue)	05:34 BST	20:24 BST

A

❧ WEATHER CHARTS ❧

Averages 1991–2020

Location

Belfast	Max temperature (°C)	12.84
	Min temperature (°C)	4.72
	Days of air frost (days)	1.34
	Sunshine (hours)	157.08
	Rainfall (mm)	60.35
	Days of rainfall ≥1 mm (days)	11.27
Cardiff	Max temperature (°C)	14.35
	Min temperature (°C)	5.73
	Days of air frost (days)	1.40
	Sunshine (hours)	176.98
	Rainfall (mm)	72.07
	Days of rainfall ≥1 mm (days)	10.73
Edinburgh	Max temperature (°C)	12.15
	Min temperature (°C)	4.70
	Days of air frost (days)	1.70
	Sunshine (hours)	157.26
	Rainfall (mm)	40.76
	Days of rainfall ≥1 mm (days)	8.63
London	Max temperature (°C)	14.13
	Min temperature (°C)	5.50
	Days of air frost (days)	1.36
	Sunshine (hours)	155.24
	Rainfall (mm)	49.59
	Days of rainfall ≥1 mm (days)	9.10

❧ TASKS ❧

Things to start

New lawns

Lawns seem to be getting a bad press – but if a lawn works for you, go for it. It's funny how patios don't seem to get the same attacks on their environmental credentials. Lawns play an important role in allowing water to escape (if you've replaced hardstanding with lawn) and play host to a wide range of insects. You don't have to use fossil fuels or electricity to keep them short (try a push mower if your lawn is small enough) and you can always leave some of it to grow long if you don't need the whole space for children's games or entertaining. The long, hot summer of 2022 should also have taught us that there's no need to water your turf to keep it alive. It will bounce back as soon as the weather cools and the rains return.

A

Herbaceous perennials

Now is the time to plant perennials. Small pots of tiny shoots are a lot cheaper than the large flowering plants you can buy in the summer, and the conditions are perfect for planting. It's warming up, but not too hot, and there is space to see what you'd like to plant where. The best time to put supports in place is when the new shoots are young. Once they've flopped, it's impossible to prop up perennials and make them look natural.

Things to finish

Asparagus

There are few more unlikely harvests to be made in the garden than the first asparagus. The first spears of the season can be ready any time from the first week in April to the first week in May (like me, asparagus struggles to keep to a schedule) depending on how quickly the weather warms up. While most vegetable crops give us a warning of their presence, the bursting of such a delicious and substantial crop from nowhere is a real gardening joy. Sever the new spears while the heads are still tight and haven't started to unfurl, making a cut below soil level. Cut off any woody stumps from last year after you harvest as these can make future harvesting tricky.

Spring cabbage

A bit like covering your car windscreen before a frosty night, having spring cabbages to harvest is one of those 'so glad I did it' moments. These dense, triangular-shaped cabbages are the ones to grow if you've been put off by soggy overcooked winter ones. Sliced strips of fresh spring cabbage added to a stir-fry are a beautiful source of natural sweetness, and just one cabbage goes a long way. They are perhaps the first heavyweight crop of the year – there's nothing 'garnish' about these brassicas. Cut them off at the base with secateurs or a sharp knife and wash them well, as little slugs have a habit of hiding inside the layers of leaves.

❧ SOMETHING TO PRUNE ❧

Lavender

You'll be so pleased you took a few minutes to cut back your lavender plants this month. A simple shearing over of the whole plant – just cutting into soft, rather than hard, wood – will keep your plants tight, compact and bushy for as long as possible. Miss just a year's pruning and lavenders can quickly become bare, woody and in need of replacement. They don't shoot readily from old wood, so if you've got a lot of leggy lavenders then it's best to start again.

❧ SOMETHING TO SAVOUR ❧

Apple blossoms

The glorious shades of pink shown off by apple trees this
month are quickly forgotten once spring is in full gear. Take
the time to enjoy these dainty blossoms, and marvel at the
fact that they will become fruit bowl staples in autumn.
Sitting out among the apple blossom on a warm April
afternoon there's a good chance you'll also enjoy a soothing
soundtrack of bees at work. Paying attention to the weather
is also a good idea, so that you can be ready with layers of
fleece to cover your apple trees if frost is forecast.

❧ THRIFTY PROJECT ❧

Home-made plant supports

Ready-made plant supports can be pretty but also pricey.
If you've got lots of perennials starting to push through
the soil, it might not be feasible to prop them all up with
stainless steel or other expensive supports. This is where the
garden keeps on giving. If you've got bamboos growing
in the garden, cut off a few canes to hold up some of your
plants. They won't be as sturdy as shop-bought ones, but they
will have a bit more bend, which makes them more versatile.
You can also use hazel stems, dogwoods or willow prunings.

HEAD GARDENER'S JOB
❧ OF THE MONTH ❧

Dividing perennials at Hidcote Manor, Gloucestershire
Head Gardener – Lottie Allen

Seventy-five years on from Lawrence Johnston's vision of Hidcote, the Red Borders are still considered to be at their best from mid-July to mid-September. These borders are an orchestra of deciduous shrubs, herbaceous perennials and grasses, tender perennials and annuals, all flowering in unison by August. As a late-flowering border, with annuals and tenders to plant, we make sure any lifting of perennials and grasses is done by May to allow for good establishment and minimal watering.

1. We loosen clumps with a fork and then lever the clump out of the ground and on to a surface that can be cleaned easily.

2. We will use a sharp spade if the growth is one compact mass or, where some plants offer a clue to the lines of least resistance, use two forks inserted back-to-back to prise the plant apart.

3. Then we plant the new clumps, making sure the buds and growth remain just proud of the soil level, and water well.

4. Swap any excess clumps with friends.

Lifting and dividing plants promotes healthy vigour, prevents dieback in the centre of the clumps and allows us to maintain the intended size of groups of plants in a border. Much like woody plants are often routinely pruned, our herbaceous perennials and grasses also need regular maintenance to look their best.

❧ PLANTS OF THE MONTH ❧

Erysimum 'Bowles's Mauve'
Few plants have the ability to be in flower every month of the year, but this evergreen perennial will come close in a sheltered, mild garden. It's visited by bees almost non-stop through the growing season and all it needs is free-draining soil and a sunny spot. It's a good idea to chop the plants back each autumn to keep them bushy, as they will eventually become leggy after a few years. Take cuttings of shoot tips in summer to raise a fresh new batch of plants. Height: 50cm (20in).

Tulipa 'Ballerina'
This deep-orange tulip adds a bright spark to the garden this month and creates vibrant colour contrasts if paired with lime-green euphorbias or azure blue pulmonarias. As well as boasting dazzling colour, 'Ballerina' has a sweet scent. You will probably be torn between enjoying it in the garden and bringing some cut stems indoors to make an easy and elegant spring centrepiece. The upright stems allow for creating a concentrated block of colour, especially if the bulbs are planted generously in a container and sited in full sun. Height: 60cm (2ft).

Epimedium 'Amber Queen'
This dainty, elegant evergreen is perfect for a woodland garden and is perhaps the antidote to bold and shouty spring bulbs. Its spider-like yellow flowers gently hang from wiry

A

stems that stand above shield-shaped leaves, which make good ground cover in dappled shade. Ideally grow it in a slightly acidic soil and mulch with rotted leaf mould each spring. Height: 45cm (18in).

❧ WILDLIFE TO LOOK FOR ❧

Orange-tip butterflies
The orange-tipped forewings of male orange-tip butterflies warns predators that this isn't a delicious meal, which is ironic given they are cannibalistic butterflies, eating their own eggshells and other orange-tip eggs they can find. The adults start to emerge from damp habitats this month, looking for nectar from flowers such as dandelions.

Red mason bees
These solitary bees, identifiable by their thick gingery hair, nest in hollow plant stems and in the crumbling mortar of old buildings. Males have white tufts on their heads whilst the females are all black in colour. After emerging from hibernation this month, the males will be first on the wing, followed later by the females. Both will be grateful for the flowers of 'Bowles's Mauve', borage and fruit tree blossom, to help replenish their fat reserves.

Bats
Hibernation will be over this month for UK bat species, such as the common pipistrelle and the brown long-eared bat. To build up their reserves they too will be on the wing, but searching instead for insects to feed on during mild evenings. They hunt and roost in areas of low light, so reducing the use of artificial lighting in the garden at night will help them.

❧ HOW TO HELP WILDLIFE ❧

Flowering currant
This shrub is an ideal choice if you want to increase the wildlife in your garden. Its vibrant leaves will add brightness to a semi-shaded spot while its clusters of pink flowers will provide much-needed nectar for bumblebees and other pollinators. Large plants can also provide nesting cover for birds.

❧ BIRDS OF THE MONTH ❧

Wren
This very small but plump and perky garden bird, with a slightly downcurved bill, is a feisty one: loud in voice and fast in flight. At the end of the month wrens start to breed, after the males have built nests. They're more likely to build nests in your garden when winters are mild and their numbers are high. Wrens will forage for spiders in low, thick vegetation, in ditches and beneath hedges, and may also eat small seeds.

Goldfinch
This colourful bird, with its red face and patch of banana-yellow plumage begins breeding towards the end of the month. Its optimistic 'chirruping' is sure to put a spring in the step of a busy, pottering gardener. Favouring rough ground, orchards and heathland, it is most common in southern England and is becoming a regular visitor to bird feeders in gardens.

❧ GARDEN EVENTS ❧

Harrogate Spring Flower Show, 18–21 April
Arguably the first major event in the garden show calendar, the show at the Great Yorkshire Showground is an exciting way to mark the arrival of spring, with spectacular exhibits from florists and nurseries, and spring show gardens.

Earth Day, 22 April
Founded in 1970, Earth Day is a time to further highlight environmental concerns, with events and activities up and down the country, from renovating local green spaces to teaching children to make their own recycled plant pots.

National Pet Month
Mark this month of celebrating and raising awareness of responsible pet ownership, by taking part in one of the dog-friendly walks at National Trust locations. There are 3,800 acres to explore at Clumber Park, and a dog-friendly cafe to take a rest in. Other dog-friendly cafes can be found at Arlington Court in North Devon and Trelissick in Cornwall. Check the National Trust website for more locations.

Toby's Garden Festival
2024 marks the 10th anniversary of this event, hosted by gardening broadcaster, Toby Buckland at Powderham Castle. Look forward to a food and drink market as well as a range of exhibits from plant nurseries, artists, designers and makers.

Fritillary Season
Celebrate the joyous spring displays of Oxfordshire's county flower at Waterperry Gardens. Fritillaries take the limelight in the wildflower meadow and the riverside walk in April.

NATIONAL TRUST GARDENS
❧ AT THEIR BEST ❧
(for bluebells)

Ashridge Estate, Hertfordshire

Situated in an area of Outstanding Natural Beauty in the Chiltern Hills, the floor of the beech and oak woodland on the Ashridge Estate is covered with a sea of beautiful bluebell flowers.

A

Blickling Estate, Norfolk

Follow the winding paths through the Great Wood and you will pass swathes of dainty bluebells while enjoying views of the spectacular hall and lake.

Trivia

There are an astonishing 15,500m (50,853ft) of yew and box hedging in the gardens at Powis Castle – that's a lot of trimmings to cut and clear up!

Emmetts Garden, Kent

The woods at this hillside garden have been designated a Site of Special Scientific Interest (SSSI) due to the incredible show of English native bluebells, which smother the hillside with a blaze of colour.

Calke Abbey, Derbyshire

With 600 acres of parkland, much of Calke is a National Nature Reserve and home to some of the oldest trees in Europe. Take a walk through the Serpentine Wood to discover a wondrous display of bluebells.

Speke Hall, Merseyside

Take a spring stroll through this green oasis on the edge of Liverpool to see inspiring displays of bluebells in Stockton's Wood, then keep walking to encounter beautiful views of the Mersey Estuary.

Trivia

The Elizabethans used the starch-like juice from the bluebell bulb to stiffen their fancy ruff collars.

_____

'A training longer than that required for a surgeon or lawyer is needed to produce a first-class head gardener.'
– Graham Stuart Thomas

_____

YOUR NOTES FOR
❧ NEXT YEAR ❧

What has worked

_____

_____

_____

_____

_____

_____

What hasn't

_____

_____

_____

_____

_____

What I'd like to try

_____

_____

_____

_____

_____

_____

_____

A

Wisteria

May

'*The greatest fine art of the future will be the making of a comfortable living from a small piece of land.*'
– Abraham Lincoln

May is the month of freshness. Soft greens, young shoots, crisp flowers and potential-packed seedlings. The sweet smell of lilac, clouds of cow parsley and globes of sparkling alliums, all amid a backdrop of light on warm evenings – it can almost feel too good to be true. As the threat of frost eases, and after weeks of waiting, it's time to unleash your home-grown vegetables and tender flowers into your plot. The garden is buzzing with life as pollinators head to the first calendulas, astrantias and poppies. Any potential problems feel on hold in May. It is a time to relish, with the added joy that summer is just around the corner.

❧ SUNRISE AND SUNSET 2024 ❧

Location	Date	Rise	Set
Belfast			
	May 01 (Wed)	05:44 BST	20:59 BST
	May 11 (Sat)	05:24 BST	21:17 BST
	May 21 (Tue)	05:08 BST	21:34 BST
	May 31 (Fri)	04:55 BST	21:48 BST
Cardiff			
	May 01 (Wed)	05:44 BST	20:37 BST
	May 11 (Sat)	05:27 BST	20:53 BST
	May 21 (Tue)	05:12 BST	21:07 BST
	May 31 (Fri)	05:02 BST	21:20 BST
Edinburgh			
	May 01 (Wed)	05:28 BST	20:53 BST
	May 11 (Sat)	05:07 BST	21:12 BST
	May 21 (Tue)	04:49 BST	21:31 BST
	May 31 (Fri)	04:36 BST	21:46 BST
London			
	May 01 (Wed)	05:32 BST	20:25 BST
	May 11 (Sat)	05:14 BST	20:41 BST
	May 21 (Tue)	05:00 BST	20:56 BST
	May 31 (Fri)	04:49 BST	21:09 BST

M

❧ WEATHER CHARTS ❧

Averages 1991–2020

Location

Belfast	Max temperature (°C)	15.74
	Min temperature (°C)	6.96
	Days of air frost (days)	0.17
	Sunshine (hours)	185.14
	Rainfall (mm)	59.63
	Days of rainfall ≥1 mm (days)	11.47
Cardiff	Max temperature (°C)	17.38
	Min temperature (°C)	8.48
	Days of air frost (days)	0.00
	Sunshine (hours)	198.37
	Rainfall (mm)	78.45
	Days of rainfall ≥1 mm (days)	11.17
Edinburgh	Max temperature (°C)	14.91
	Min temperature (°C)	7.08
	Days of air frost (days)	0.37
	Sunshine (hours)	194.66
	Rainfall (mm)	47.60
	Days of rainfall ≥1 mm (days)	9.63
London	Max temperature (°C)	17.33
	Min temperature (°C)	8.30
	Days of air frost (days)	0.03
	Sunshine (hours)	199.18
	Rainfall (mm)	50.51
	Days of rainfall ≥1 mm (days)	8.52

❧ TASKS ❧

Things to start

Tender plants

It's hard to be patient when it comes to planting out tender plants. There are so many exciting, vibrant plants waiting to be planted out into the garden. Not planting them when you want to is like a child having to wait until Christmas Day to open their presents. Hold off though, because a couple of extra days indoors can be a life-or-death matter for a courgette. Choose a still, mild day for planting out tender plants and get supports in early when you plant. Water thoroughly and spread a 5cm (2in) layer of well-rotted or bagged compost around the base of the plant. This can save you a lot of effort watering in summer.

Salads from seed

Growing your own salad so you have a constant, fresh supply requires discipline. Little and often is the key to enjoying a steady supply of crunchy lettuce. Try sowing two seeds per module in a six-cell tray – kept at 20°C (68°F) indoors – every three weeks and you should avoid having 20 lettuces to eat one week, then none for the next six. In the soil outside, sow short rows of rocket, peas for pea shoots and loose-leaved lettuce every three weeks in a sunny spot for a steady supply of a tastier, more varied salad.

Things to finish

Spring bulb aftercare

Once flowering is over it's only natural to forget about spring bulbs (how fickle gardeners can be, when we were so glad of them only a short time ago), but a little attention before the foliage dies down will pay dividends in giving a

M

good show next spring. Leave daffodils untouched for six weeks before cutting them down or mowing over them, and water with a liquid, high-potassium plant food, to enhance the bulbs' reserves for next year. This will help prevent bulb blindness.

Spring onions

Onions planted as sets in autumn are now developing quickly. Pulling some of the crop early in spring gives a delicious harvest of spring onions. Then, let the rest of the bulbs mature into heavyweight 'maincrop' onions, to be harvested in August and September. Make your final harvest of spring onions by removing any plants that are close to another, to give the remaining plants room to develop into good-sized onions.

❧ SOMETHING TO PRUNE ❧

Late-flowering perennials

Perennials such as sedum, *Verbena bonariensis*, helenium and phlox can be trimmed back now to make stockier, bushier plants that produce sideshoots that give extra flowers. Flower growth will be smaller and delayed, but there will be more. Cut the stems back by up to half. If you've got more than one clump of the same plant, cut some down but not others, to stretch the flowering season.

❧ SOMETHING TO SAVOUR ❧

The choices at your fingertips

May is the month when so many edible plants can be started, whether it's buying a few chillies and peppers in pots, or sowing a fresh row of peas or carrots. Make the most of the opportunity by sowing or planting as many crops as you can. By mid-June, time will be quickly running out to begin growing crops from scratch and still be able to harvest them by the end of the season.

❧ THRIFTY PROJECT ❧

Make comfrey food

Comfrey leaves can be used to make a nutritious plant food that is high in potassium, bringing you a step closer to gardening organically. Comfrey may establish as a weed in domestic gardens when dropped by birds for example, but you can buy seeds too and sow them directly into the soil over the next two months to still harvest this year. Comfrey leaves could also work as a 'slug decoy' if left on the ground in front of vulnerable plants. To make comfrey plant food:

1. Finely chop up young comfrey leaves (not the stems) and put them in a clean bucket.

2. Press the leaves down with a brick or some pieces of rubble and add water so the leaves are just covered.

3. Cover the bucket with a lid and leave it for at least three weeks, then dilute with one part comfrey mix to ten parts water.

4. Keep the liquid food in an airtight container because it has a very pungent aroma.

HEAD GARDENER'S JOB
❧ OF THE MONTH ❦

Feeding and mulching plants at Trengwainton, Cornwall
Head Gardener – Catrina Saunders

The garden at Trengwainton is set on a sheltered coastal site near
Penzance and hosts one of the Trust's finest collections of exotic
and woodland plants, including a vast number of tree ferns.

In the woodland garden, where the huge rhododendrons grow,
we don't need to feed and mulch because we leave the fallen
leaves and the soil undisturbed, and the natural soil process of
nutrient recycling works well. But in the more formal areas,
where we clear leaves, the extra nutrients from organic material
are much appreciated by our plants. Our palms like to be fed in
May – by then the soil has warmed up enough for them to be
able to absorb the nutrients that are being put down.

For many plants, a general fertiliser is good enough, but for palms,
we use a specific feed that has magnesium in it, and for camellias,
we use plant foods that are low in nitrogen. After feeding we cover
the area with an organic mulch – compost, or very well-rotted
manure – to a depth of 5-7cm (2–3in). It's best not to pile it up
next to the trunks, as plants have only two ways to cope with this
– root into the material, or rot away, and neither of those are ideal.

Feeding and mulching plants this month gives them a supply
of nutrients for growth and helps keeps the root zone protected
from drought and heat. This means our displays of exotic trees
and shrubs at Trengwainton are still spectacular in the hottest
summer spells. This is especially important as we experience
progressively hot and dry summers.

❧ PLANTS OF THE MONTH ❧

Geranium 'Rozanne'
This violet-blue hardy geranium is sterile, which means that it just keeps on flowering from now until well into the autumn, giving you a pocket of early summer colour for months. It's a sprawling grower, but a light trim in midsummer will keep it in check, and there will still be more blooms in autumn. Grow it in any soil except boggy soil, and in sun or semi-shade. Height: 60cm (2ft).

Wisteria
Both species of wisteria commonly grown in Great Britain (*Wisteria sinensis* and *W. floribunda*) will form woody stems like tree trunks over time, the former in an anticlockwise direction, the latter clockwise. This makes a sturdy structure necessary. A south- or west-facing aspect is best and a monthly feed with a high-potassium plant food in the growing season is ideal. If space is tight, you could train a wisteria as a standard and grow it in a large container of soil-based compost. Height: 9m (27ft).

Peony 'Sarah Bernhardt'
This ruffled double-flowered variety is a classic and much-loved peony. The crisp pink blooms have a silver tint and are held on long stems. This makes them a superb cut flower, although it may be too much of a wrench to remove them from the garden. Grow in deep, well-drained soil in a sunny place. Height: 1m (40in).

❧ WILDLIFE TO LOOK FOR ᕙ

Large red damselfly
The first damselflies of the year to emerge in Britain, red
damselflies can be spotted at pond edges this month. The
males are red and black, and the females almost entirely black.
They can also be found in grassy areas and around woodland.

Common blue butterfly
The male common blue butterfly is found in woodland,
grassy meadows, large gardens and waste ground. The name
refers to the adult males, with bright blue wings, a brown
edge and white fringe. Females are brown with orange spots
on the undersides of their wings. In May, the caterpillars
will feed on wild plants such as bird's foot trefoil and
white clover.

Hoverflies
There are more than 280 species of hoverfly in Britain,
similar in appearance to wasps and honeybees, but they do
not bite or sting. Their larvae are excellent at reducing aphid
populations and also feed on whiteflies and scale insects.
Adult hoverflies like to pollinate plants with open blooms
such as calendula, poppies and alliums.

❧ HOW TO HELP WILDLIFE ᕙ

Make insect habitats with logs
If space in the garden is tight, create a small stack of material
in a sunny corner to encourage a variety of wildlife. Group
together some sawn logs and drill holes in the ends. Include
a few bricks with holes in the centre, twigs, tubes filled with

corrugated cardboard and, if possible, stuff straw in between each item. Cover the pile with black polythene or a large piece of wood to keep it dry. Ideally site the pile around a piece of overgrown grass.

❧ BIRDS OF THE MONTH ❧

Siskin
If you have conifers in your garden then you may come across siskins. These slender finches with yellow and black wings are fond of the seeds of pines and spruces, although they may also visit your bird feeders to snack on some peanuts. They build tiny nests in the tops of trees and are most frequently found in Wales and Scotland.

M

Swift
Eating, sleeping, bathing and mating on the wing, this bird truly lives life in the fast lane, capable of flying close to 70 miles per hour. Rarely touching the ground, you are most likely to see a swift in the garden as something of a black blur, although they are brown with a white throat. Swifts mate for life and return to the same site each year, with a preference for the eaves of old buildings.

❧ GARDEN EVENTS ❧

British Tomato Fortnight, 20 May–2 June
Hopefully this will serve as a reminder to either plant out your tomatoes, buy some plants, or remember to water and feed the ones that are already in place.

RHS Chelsea Flower Show, 21–25 May
The world-famous flower show returns with another spectacular line up of breath-taking show gardens and meticulously curated exhibits from plant nurseries.

National Children's Gardening Week, 25 May–2 June
Gardening with children is both a wonderful learning experience and a way to discover new levels of patience that you didn't know you had! Time spent in the garden showing children how to grow plants is an investment in their lives that cannot be underestimated.

Water Saving Week, 27–31 May
Dry UK summers can make gardening a challenge. This week is a chance to engage with the different ways that you can save water in the garden.

Scotney Flower Festival
Celebrate the arrival of May with a visit to the annual flower festival at Scotney Castle, Kent. The house is filled with special themed displays of flowers created by flower groups, church groups, local schools and colleges.

RHS Malvern Spring Festival
This spring festival features exceptional displays of spring plants by leading nurseries, gardening talks and demonstrations by well-known gardeners and chefs, as well as lots of opportunities to buy plants and local artisan crafts.

NATICKAL TRUST GARDENS
❧ AT THEIR BEST ❧
(to see wisteria)

Nymans, West Sussex
Wisterias clamber the walls of the house and the ruins in the Knot Garden in late spring creating the most romantic backdrop.

Powys Castle, Welshpool
The wonderfully floriferous *Wisteria floribunda* on the Aviary Terrace is the most spectacular herald of summer at Powys Castle. The plant is thought to be over 180 years old.

M

Greys Court, Oxfordshire
The magnificent wisteria walk at Grey's Court envelops you in its special blooms as they hang to decorate tunnels and pergolas, with the fourteenth-century country house in view.

Goddards, Yorkshire
Relax on a bench and take in the beautiful scene of this charming Arts and Crafts house, former home of the chocolate-making Terry family, strewn with wisteria, with the formal pond and fountain in the foreground.

Trivia
Shaw's Corner in Hertfordshire was home to playwright George Bernard Shaw from 1906 to 1950. He called his writing hut in the garden 'London' so that when he didn't want to be disturbed his house staff could truthfully turn down enquiries with 'I'm afraid Mr Shaw is in London'.

Knightshayes, Devon

A beautiful garden of imaginatively shaped topiary, sculpture, and artistically clipped hedges, there is so much to see at Knightshayes, but make sure you seek out a tremendous pair of aged standard wisterias.

'A weed is a plant that has mastered every skill except for learning how to grow in rows.'
– Doug Larson

YOUR NOTES FOR
∾ NEXT YEAR ∾

What has worked

_____
_____
_____
_____
_____
_____

What hasn't

_____
_____
_____
_____
_____

What I'd like to try

_____
_____
_____
_____
_____
_____
_____

M

Strawberry plant

June

'*The garden year has
no beginning and no end.*'
– Elizabeth Lawrence

June is a month of heady scents, sweet fruits, luscious blooms and the end of the 'hungry gap' – meaning lots of summer vegetables are becoming ready to harvest. There is no better month to be a gardener. The evenings are warm and the results of earlier planting and sowing begin to appear. In June, that perfect balance between gardening busyness and sitting back and enjoying the garden is easier to achieve than at any other time of year. Still, it's hard not to look back at pictures and think that you took that enticing mix of warmth, colour and abundance for granted. Take some time to step back and soak in the atmosphere of the garden this month. It's delicious while it lasts.

❧ SUNRISE AND SUNSET 2024 ❦

Location	Date	Rise	Set
Belfast			
	Jun 01 (Sat)	04:55 BST	21:50 BST
	Jun 11 (Tue)	04:48 BST	22:00 BST
	Jun 21 (Fri)	04:47 BST	22:04 BST
	Jun 30 (Sun)	04:52 BST	22:03 BST
Cardiff			
	Jun 01 (Sat)	05:01 BST	21:21 BST
	Jun 11 (Tue)	04:56 BST	21:30 BST
	Jun 21 (Fri)	04:56 BST	21:34 BST
	Jun 30 (Sun)	05:00 BST	21:33 BST
Edinburgh			
	Jun 01 (Sat)	04:35 BST	21:47 BST
	Jun 11 (Tue)	04:28 BST	21:58 BST
	Jun 21 (Fri)	04:27 BST	22:03 BST
	Jun 30 (Sun)	04:31 BST	22:01 BST
London			
	Jun 01 (Sat)	04:49 BST	21:10 BST
	Jun 11 (Tue)	04:43 BST	21:18 BST
	Jun 21 (Fri)	04:43 BST	21:23 BST
	Jun 30 (Sun)	04:47 BST	21:22 BST

J

❧ WEATHER CHARTS ❧

Averages 1991–2020

Location

Belfast	Max temperature (°C)	18.19
	Min temperature (°C)	9.72
	Days of air frost (days)	0.00
	Sunshine (hours)	151.09
	Rainfall (mm)	68.95
	Days of rainfall ≥1 mm (days)	11.44
Cardiff	Max temperature (°C)	20.07
	Min temperature (°C)	11.27
	Days of air frost (days)	0.00
	Sunshine (hours)	195.21
	Rainfall (mm)	73.54
	Days of rainfall ≥1 mm (days)	10.37
Edinburgh	Max temperature (°C)	17.43
	Min temperature (°C)	9.93
	Days of air frost (days)	0.00
	Sunshine (hours)	161.81
	Rainfall (mm)	66.21
	Days of rainfall ≥1 mm (days)	10.40
London	Max temperature (°C)	20.38
	Min temperature (°C)	11.17
	Days of air frost (days)	0.00
	Sunshine (hours)	193.67
	Rainfall (mm)	58.45
	Days of rainfall ≥1 mm (days)	8.73

❧ TASKS ❧

Things to start

Hanging baskets

There's still time to plant up some hanging baskets. In June, tender annual plants can be planted out more or less anywhere in Britain without fear of frost. A layer of fleece can be draped over the top of plants if a very late frost is forecast. Make sure that the brackets are secure before hanging your baskets. For a more permanent display, consider planting your basket solely with hardy plants. Periwinkles (vinca) are good trailing plants that can flower in any month of the year, and carex make good, structural evergreen plants. *Sempervivums* and hardy succulents such as *Sedum acre* – hardy to -10°C (14°F) – are good choices for a drought-tolerant basket display.

J

Compost heap

With extra warmth and green waste available in the garden this month, it's a great time to start composting. To make the perfect compost you need the right mix of ingredients. Half should be soft 'green' material, such as grass clippings, kitchen peelings or annual weeds like chickweed. The other half is best made up of 'brown' material, such as hedge clippings, ripped-up egg boxes, shredded paper, plant stems and fallen leaves. Too much green and you will end up with a slimy airless mass. Too much brown and the materials won't break down well enough to make a fine texture. Avoid putting meat or cooked food in the compost as it can attract rodents. If you want to recycle all of your food waste, consider investing in a wormery. Also, refrain from composting perennial weeds and diseased leaves, as they can linger in the heap to cause trouble later. Lay a few twiggy branches on the bottom when starting a new batch of compost. This allows for good airflow at the bottom and will make it easy to turn. Placing either a bin or a heap over bare earth, rather than a hard standing container, is ideal, so that worms can get to work on breaking down the material.

Things to finish

New potatoes
If early varieties of potato planted in early spring are in flower, then it's time for an exciting moment: checking for buried treasure. If you have small children, the excitement goes up an extra notch. Ask them to stand back as you sink a fork into the ground and lift it up to reveal the harvest (they'll never want to watch TV on a summer's afternoon again). If you are unsure if the crop is ready, loosen the soil at the base of one plant with a hand fork and feel for any tubers with your hands. Leave it another week or so if they feel too small. Harvest new potatoes as and when you want them, for maximum freshness.

Strawberries
Picking strawberries to add to porridge for breakfast is one of my all-time favourite summer events (sorry Wimbledon). To have soft, sun-warmed strawberries 'on tap' from the garden is one of the real joys of growing your own food – their taste and texture indistinguishable from the pale, woody imitations sold in supermarkets. Pick over your plant thoroughly, removing any spoilt fruits and those pecked by birds. Pull out any weeds you see and then put the netting back after picking.

❧ SOMETHING TO PRUNE ❧

Early summer-flowering shrubs

Shrubs that are glorious in May but fading towards the
second half of June include deutzia, weigela, philadelphus
and kolkwitzia. If you have any of these plants and they are
starting to look a bit ungainly, trim them now so they have
time to put on new growth that will bear next year's flowers.
Prune any dead or damaged stems and remove some of the
thicker ones at ground level in plants that are congested.
Remove any thin and spindly shoots, and reduce the height
of any stems that are outgrowing their space, cutting back to
just above the bud.

❧ SOMETHING TO SAVOUR ❧

J

Fresh herbs

There are so many delightful perfumes in the garden at this
time of year that it's easy to overlook herbs. This month sees
soft, pungent new growth everywhere, offering sumptuous
flavour, whether you're looking for mint to complete a
cocktail or fresh chives to add some extra flavour to a salad.
The added bonus of snipping new shoots from your herbs
is that it will encourage bushier growth for the rest of the
season. You may want to hold off on cutting thyme until after
it has bloomed, to enjoy the flowering display.

The first fresh peas

Is there a sweeter taste than the first homegrown peas of
the year? Do any of yours make it back to the kitchen? Not
many of mine do! Pick them when the pods are plump but
still smooth, and before the peas have gone almost square

shaped. Then you have a delicacy that makes a summer morning's pottering in the garden extra special. Make sure to check the lower part of the plant – it's easy to miss a few pods that have become tangled up in netting or hidden by their own foliage. While you savour the taste of early varieties such as 'Early Onward' or 'Avola' it's also time to take advantage of their quick maturing nature and sow another batch, which will establish fast for an extra crop later in summer. The picking season lasts several weeks for one batch of peas and it's easy to forget to get another batch ready from seed, but you'll be so glad you did.

✧ THRIFTY PROJECT ✧

Recycled labels

With the potential for lots of comings and goings to the
veg patch, having clear labels will make life a lot easier.
It will help prevent bare ground from being sown by accident
while initial sowings are still below ground, and will also help
you to easily identify seedlings. The following materials can
be recycled into plant labels. Make sure to write the plant
names in waterproof, UV-resistant marker pen:

- Timber offcuts
- Lolly sticks
- Large corks with a wooden skewer inserted
- Skewers with duct tape folded at the top to make
  a flag
- Sturdy twigs with the seed packet pierced into the
  top of it (indoors)
- Large stones

J

'You can bury any number
of headaches in the garden.'
– Charles Barnard

HEAD GARDENER'S JOB
❧ OF THE MONTH ❧

Staking dahlias at Biddulph Grange, Staffordshire
Head Gardener – Paul Walton

Biddulph Grange is a Grade 1-listed garden and is cleverly designed with hedges and banks to form hidden rooms. One of these rooms is the Dahlia Walk.

The Dahlia Walk is one of the main summer displays and is divided into nine sections with upper and lower levels. In early June, we put in around 600 stakes to support the dahlias. We space the stakes evenly, forming straight rows to ensure a formal planting display. The stakes are of varying heights with 1.8m (6ft) stakes put at the back, and 90cm (3ft) ones at the front. Once planted, this forms a neat, tiered effect. The plants can become top heavy when in full flower, so we advise using a stake rather than a cane. This ensures that the plants are supported well and keeps the display neat and tidy.

The Dahlia Walk is a mass of colour in late summer and the stakes continue to support the plants even with some varieties getting over 1.8m (6ft) tall. The stakes are square rather than round, so the string used to support the plants remains in place throughout the season.

❧ PLANTS OF THE MONTH ❧

Rose 'The Pilgrim'

Now is the time when most roses announce themselves
with a first flush of blooms, and few are finer than this
charming climber which flowers all through summer.
A luscious lemon yellow in the centre, fading to cream at
the edges, the many petalled blooms form flat rosettes as
they age, standing up well to rainfall. It's almost thornless,
so the stems are very easy to train around a pillar or up an
obelisk. Height: 3.6m (12ft).

Alchemilla epipsila

Perhaps the perfect companion to plant in front of roses,
this compact form of Lady's mantle is not such a rampant
self-seeder as the more widely grown *Alchemilla mollis*, so
it's easier to control. It has the trademark plumes of frothy
yellowy-green flowers: delicate, star-shaped and born in
clusters on airy, branching stems. Height: 30cm (12in).

Astrantia 'Roma'

This perky perennial is both easy and elegant, one of the
most reliably slug-proof plants for the border. The sturdy
stems make for long-lasting cut flowers and the flowers
will lighten up the garden from May until August. Grow
it in soil that drains well, in full sun or dappled shade.
Height: 60cm (2ft).

J

❧ WILDLIFE TO LOOK FOR ❧

Eyed ladybird
This hefty ladybird is the largest type in the UK. It's easily recognisable not only due to its size, but also its distinctive yellow rings around its black spots. Around 10mm (0.4in) in length, it is commonly seen on pine trees. Both the adults and the larvae will eat aphids.

Hummingbird hawkmoth
This moth is the closest you'll get to seeing a hummingbird on these shores, and is most active between June and September. It has brown forewings and orange hindwings that produce a hum as they beat so rapidly. You're most likely to see it on a sunny summer afternoon, because of its preference for flying in bright sunlight and attraction to nectar-rich plants such as honeysuckle, phlox and lilac.

Slugs
On wet nights, it can seem like an army of these leaf-munching molluscs descend on the garden. Yet if it's a dry June, it's easy to forget that slugs exist all, especially if your soil is on the free-draining, stony side. Slugs live in dark, damp places or beneath the soil surface, and need constant moisture to survive. Most slugs are herbivores, but the leopard slug, with its distinctive leopard-like patterning, will eat other slugs. It is impossible to eradicate slugs completely, but you can create a

'slug decoy' to entice them away from vulnerable plants. Leave out slates or tiles with old lettuce leaves to build a habitat that they will love (hopefully more than your veg plot).

❧ HOW TO HELP WILDLIFE ❧

Add butterfly-friendly plants to hanging baskets placed in full sun, to make your garden as attractive as possible to wildlife. Basket favourites such as trailing lobelia and white alyssum are great, as are near-constant flowering calibrachoas, which are also drought-tolerant. Trailing ivies will be a late nectar source for butterflies too.

❧ BIRDS OF THE MONTH ❧

J

House martin
It's happy hour again for house martins when the weather is warm and sunny and there are plenty of flying insects to take back to their nests. They start arriving in the UK from Africa in April before heading to warmer climes in October. While on our shores, they commonly make nests built of mud in the eaves of houses (hence the name) or sheds, and often return to them in following years.

Dunnock
Sometimes called the hedge sparrow, this small, robin-sized bird is most likely to be seen at ground level in sheltered places, moving gingerly as it searches for insects and worms. They are nervous birds, unless males come into contact with one another – then they will both call loudly and flick their wings to claim territory. This brown and grey bird nests in hedges and shrubs, and its call is a wonderfully calming 'chirrup'.

❧ GARDEN EVENTS ❧

National Growing for Wellbeing Week
A celebration of how growing your own produce can improve your physical and mental wellbeing. Launched by the Life at No.27 gardening blog, resources are available from www.lifeatno27.com

Rose Awareness Week, 17–23 June
A week to highlight the garden versatility of roses, with the chance to discover how best to grow garden roses. The National Trust has many rose gardens you can visit to celebrate the week (see opposite) and they have recently launched a new rose 'Mottisfont', named after the famous garden in Hampshire.

The Blenheim Palace Flower Show
Set in more than 2,000 acres of parkland, this three-day event is a celebration of the best of British gardening, with quality plants in the Grand Floral Pavilion, outdoor floral displays, gardening talks, and fabulous food and drink.

BBC Gardeners' World Live
Get close to the much-loved TV programme at this exhibition show packed with beautiful gardens, advice from favourite presenters and gardening experts, and a wide range of nurseries exhibiting and selling plants.

Bord Bia Bloom
A massive show, taking place over 70 acres of Phoenix Park, Dublin, highlighting the best of Irish horticulture, food and drink, with show gardens, postcard gardens, nursery displays and many local food and drink outlets.

NATIONAL TRUST GARDENS
❧ AT THEIR BEST ❦
(for roses)

Barrington Court, Somerset

The main rose garden here was originally designed by Gertrude Jekyll in the 1920s. The rose beds were refreshed in 2017, following Jekyll's scheme by including rose varieties as close as possible to the colours that she originally chose.

Trivia
Wightwick Manor has a cat flap on the first floor, which Lady Mander's cat used to access by climbing up the wisteria on the west wing of the house.

Chartwell, Kent

There are two very special places to see an abundance of roses at Chartwell: the Golden Rose Avenue and Lady Clementine's Rose Garden. Running through the centre of the garden, the Avenue was planted in 1958, originally with standard roses. Lady Clementine's is a traditional rose garden of four beds divided by paths.

Mottisfont, Hampshire

A real paradise for rose aficionados, restored by the National Trust's legendary plantsman Graham Stuart Thomas, with more than 500 varieties of rose in bloom in the magnificent Walled Garden. Mottisfont is home to the National Collection of pre-1900 old-fashioned roses, which save all their energy for one glorious flush of flowers, each June. 2024 is a particularly special year to visit Mottisfont as it will be celebrating the 50th anniversary of the Rose Garden.

The Argory, Co Armagh
There is something of a fairytale feel to this rose garden, with billowing pink blossom dripping from standard roses, housed in rose beds edged deeply with curvy box hedging.

Trivia
The garden at Chastleton House contains box plants shaped as chess pieces that date back to the 1820s.

Compton Castle, Devon
Enclosed by stone walls, with climbers covering pillars and pergolas, this romantic garden mixes roses with lavender, peonies and clematis, to create a riot of colour and perfume in June.

'Bread and roses! Bread and roses!
Our lives shall not be sweated from
birth until life closes;
Hearts starve as well as bodies;
give us bread, but give us roses.'
– James Oppenheim

YOUR NOTES FOR
❧ NEXT YEAR ❧

What has worked

_____

_____

_____

_____

_____

_____

What hasn't

_____

_____

_____

_____

_____

What I'd like to try

_____

_____

_____

_____

_____

_____

_____

_____

J

Red admiral butterfly on a buddleja

July

'July arrives with a lived-in, worldly air that is something of a relief after all the bustling vigour of spring and early summer.'
– Monty Don

July is the month of rapid maturity. Crops seem to change overnight, as do weeds if given half a chance. New flowers are bursting open every day. Hot days are both a time to bask and enjoy the frenetic activity of butterflies and to slake the thirst of plants that can flag in the hot sun. In July, we learn a lot about our gardens. Are we too dependent on hungry and thirsty plants? Have we left enough room for them, now that they are spreading out? Have we sown enough summer flowers? Whatever the answer, there is so much to enjoy because a garden in July is very forgiving. Warm nights, warm soil, warm colours. See it as a beautiful place, whatever its condition.

❧ SUNRISE AND SUNSET 2024 ❦

Location	Date	Rise	Set
Belfast			
	Jul 01 (Mon)	04:52 BST	22:03 BST
	Jul 11 (Thu)	05:03 BST	21:55 BST
	Jul 21 (Sun)	05:17 BST	21:42 BST
	Jul 31 (Wed)	05:33 BST	21:26 BST
Cardiff			
	Jul 01 (Mon)	05:00 BST	21:33 BST
	Jul 11 (Thu)	05:09 BST	21:27 BST
	Jul 21 (Sun)	05:21 BST	21:16 BST
	Jul 31 (Wed)	05:36 BST	21:02 BST
Edinburgh			
	Jul 01 (Mon)	04:32 BST	22:01 BST
	Jul 11 (Thu)	04:43 BST	21:53 BST
	Jul 21 (Sun)	04:58 BST	21:39 BST
	Jul 31 (Wed)	05:16 BST	21:21 BST
London			
	Jul 01 (Mon)	04:48 BST	21:22 BST
	Jul 11 (Thu)	04:57 BST	21:16 BST
	Jul 21 (Sun)	05:09 BST	21:05 BST
	Jul 31 (Wed)	05:23 BST	20:50 BST

J

❧ WEATHER CHARTS ❧

Averages 1991–2020

Location		
Belfast	Max temperature (°C)	19.73
	Min temperature (°C)	11.56
	Days of air frost (days)	0.00
	Sunshine (hours)	146.31
	Rainfall (mm)	73.62
	Days of rainfall ≥1 mm (days)	13.00
Cardiff	Max temperature (°C)	21.79
	Min temperature (°C)	13.12
	Days of air frost (days)	0.00
	Sunshine (hours)	199.56
	Rainfall (mm)	83.58
	Days of rainfall ≥1 mm (days)	11.23
Edinburgh	Max temperature (°C)	19.29
	Min temperature (°C)	11.60
	Days of air frost (days)	0.00
	Sunshine (hours)	169.93
	Rainfall (mm)	72.06
	Days of rainfall ≥1 mm (days)	11.47
London	Max temperature (°C)	22.73
	Min temperature (°C)	13.34
	Days of air frost (days)	0.00
	Sunshine (hours)	199.79
	Rainfall (mm)	50.49
	Days of rainfall ≥1 mm (days)	8.43

❧ TASKS ❦

Things to start

Asian greens and vegetables

These salads are a real gift in summer and are an easy way
to increase the supply of fresh leaves you can harvest from
the garden. They are daylight-sensitive, best sown after the
longest day, when they are less prone to bolting. If they do
bolt though, all parts of the plant are still edible, so it's no
loss. Grow brown mustard to give a mixed salad a 'mustardy'
kick, or for something crunchy for a stir fry, bok choy is a
classic, which you can also harvest as soft baby leaves. Choose
a semi-shaded spot in soil that holds onto moisture well.
Avoid growing these crops in soil that receives a lot of sun.

Late-flowering perennials to plug gaps

J

Summer planting might not be recommended very often
– if the temperature is above 20°C (68°F), it's not the ideal
time to plant – but don't be put off adding new plants this
month. A trip to the garden centre can tell you what's in
flower and how it can work in your garden, especially if you
can see gaps in space and colour. If it's hot and sunny, and no
rain is forecast, you can keep plants in their pots in shade and
keep them damp until the weather eases off. Soak them after
planting and apply a 5cm (2in) mulch. If the soil dries out
give them another drink and repeat when necessary.

Harvesting runner beans

If you don't think that you can grow tropical plants but you
grow runner beans, then you can. The first fresh runner
beans of summer are something of a milestone in the
gardening year. The time for youth and promise is being

replaced by adulthood and end results, with the harvest continuing for a good two months. Check the plants every couple of days and pick the pods when they are still light green in colour, and before the beans are becoming noticeable inside the pod. Keep the roots damp and cool by mulching well with rotted compost after watering, if the soil is dry.

Things to finish

Garlic

It's been a long road from planting bulbs on a cold November day to pulling pungent, fat necks of garlic on an idyllic summer's afternoon. The crop is ready to harvest when the leaves turn yellow, which can be variable, depending on the amount of moisture in the soil. Carefully lift the bulbs, pulling by the foliage to release them from the ground. Lay them out on a tray and place on a sunny windowsill or in a greenhouse for a couple of weeks, until the leaves have completely dried out. Then cut off the leaf stalk and store at 10°C (50°F).

'Gardening is full of mistakes, almost all of them pleasant and some of them actually instructive.'
– Henry Mitchell

❧ SOMETHING TO PRUNE ❧

Hebes

Tightly packed, bushy hebes are underrated in the garden,
providing form, flowers and food for insects. Large, looser
forms such as 'Silver Queen' are good for large mixed
borders, while smaller, tighter ones such as 'Emerald Gem'
can be clipped to make a low formal hedge or topiary
domes. As hebe flowers start to fade, trim the stem back to
soft leafy growth, cutting just above the leaf. Keep this up
every summer and you will avoid the stems getting bare and
woody. Once the plants are woody, they don't shoot readily
from old, thick stems.

❧ SOMETHING TO SAVOUR ❧

Cut roses for the house

It may seem a shame to cut roses from the garden (especially
if plants are young and the flowers are not yet plentiful)
but it's such a treat to have a few fresh blooms in the house.
Even a handful of cut roses, with the flowers about to unfurl
from a 'buttonhole' shape, makes an elegant and stylish table
centrepiece. Arrange the flowers in short vases if you don't
want to lose a lot of height from your rose bushes at this
time of year.

Scent-filled sweet peas

Keep on snipping and sniffing these delightful flowers, which
will be smothering the plants this month as they reach the
top of their supports. Admire them as you walk around the
garden and take time to enjoy the generosity of summer.
Then snip off the fresh sweet pea flowers to ensure that they

J

keep pumping out colour for the rest of the season. Just a few days of missed snipping can result in the plants running out of steam by the end of the month.

❧ THRIFTY PROJECT ❧

Semi-ripe cuttings
The new growth on shrubs and shrubby perennials such as *Erysimum*, *Artemisia*, *Escallonia* and lavender is starting to firm up this month and is suitable material for taking cuttings.

1. Trim off some healthy new shoots using sharp secateurs, and put them straight into a clear plastic bag kept out of direct sun.

2. Prepare the cuttings straight away, trimming them to 15cm (6in) and making a clean cut at the base with a cuttings knife, just below a leaf joint.

3. Remove the lowest pair of leaves and the tip, then insert the cuttings around the edge of 10cm (4in) pots filled with gritty compost, so they are not touching each other, and the leaves are not in touch with the compost.

4. Water once, then keep the cuttings in a greenhouse or propagator, or cover the pot with a clear plastic bag secured with an elastic band.

HEAD GARDENER'S JOB
❧ OF THE MONTH ❦

**Preparing late-summer displays at Cragside, Northumberland
Head Gardener – Peter Edge**

Cragside was the first place in the world to be lit with hydroelectricity. William Armstrong used the grounds as a vast testing site to harness the power of water. With his wife, Margaret, they built their home and transformed a rocky moorland into a fantasy mountain landscape. Nestled within the grounds is the Formal Garden – a vibrant ornamental garden that was filled with plants and flowers from all over the world. While the garden has changed over time, the gardeners continue to plant with masses of bold colours in mind.

At the start of summer, we plant the dahlia display. By July, these should be growing well but not yet flowering. They require plenty of nutrients, so we will feed them and ensure the borders are weed-free, as well as start to tie them to formal stakes this month. We will also pinch out the top growing tip, known as 'stopping', to encourage late-summer branching and a proliferation of flowers. We also plant our summer bedding borders with plants such as pelargoniums, verbena and cineraria. These are fed monthly with organic chicken manure pellets, which are easy to apply with little risk of damaging the foliage.

These late-summer flower displays are a key feature of Cragside. They offer a wonderful surprise of colour as autumn approaches, exciting the senses, contrasting with the wilder areas of the grounds. In July, work will ensure that a mass of flowers will show more vibrantly and for a longer period, from August right through until the first frost.

❧ PLANTS OF THE MONTH ❧

Echinacea

There are so many colours and flower forms of Echinacea
available to gardeners these days – much more than there were
a generation ago. The more fancy forms tend to be the fussiest
and the secret to successful growth is sharp drainage. Grow
them in full sun for the best flowering and keep them well
watered in the first couple of years. Their tolerance to drought
is low until they're well established. Leave flowerheads intact
for winter structure. Height: up to 1.5m (5ft).

Calibrachoa Million Bells Terracotta

One of the most elegant trailing summer bedding plants, the
terracotta-streaked and light orange blooms of *Calibrachoa*
(Million Bells) 'Terracotta' keep coming all summer long. A
'self-cleaning' plant, it sheds its old flowers so there's no need
to deadhead. It copes well with drought. Height: 10cm (4in).

Achillea 'Cerise Queen'

The delightful mix of bold, flat flowerheads and soft,
feathery foliage make achilleas a must-have for sunny
borders with 'thin', sandy soil. This is a tremendous plant for
providing sharp colour to a sun-baked spot in the garden.
Stake the plants well and the clusters of flowers will provide
blocks of colour in the middle of a border, as well as being
good landing pads for pollinators. Height: 60cm (2ft).

Nicotiana sylvestris

Looking somewhat ungainly from a distance, the flowers of this
fast-growing annual prove to be elegant on closer inspection, and
at night they release a sweet, delicious scent. With such a heady
fragrance to be enjoyed, grow it close to a seating area or back or

front door so that the perfume is regularly savoured. Flowering from July to October after a spring sowing, deadheading encourages more blooms and they make good cut flowers too. Height: 1.5m (5ft).

❧ WILDLIFE TO LOOK FOR ❧

Leafcutter bees
These insects will turn some of the leaves on your rose bushes into works of art, cutting perfectly shaped notches out of them. See them not as pests but as artists – their life's work, taking leaf material back to their nests to make cells for larvae to live in, does little to harm your plants.

Red admirals
Surely one of the most well-known butterflies to grace our gardens, the red admiral is a common sight this month as migrants arrive from North Africa and Europe to lay eggs in the spring. Buddlejas – try a sterile one such as 'Miss Ruby' to stop unwanted self-seeding – are a favourite plant, but the butterflies will be flying until the end of autumn, when ivy flowers and fallen fruit make ideal feeding stations.

J

Ants
Ants are rarely a problem in gardens and any nuisance they cause is easily solved. If you end up with an anthill in the lawn, brush away the excess soil on a dry day, and firm it down. Ants can potentially disturb the roots of young plants, but simply firm in and water well to re-secure them. Ants prefer dry conditions, so keeping plants well-watered and mulched will reduce the risk of harm. Ants are on the lookout for honeydew (sticky residue left behind by aphids), so they will protect aphids from predators. Keeping on top of aphids will reduce an influx of ants.

❧ HOW TO HELP WILDLIFE ❧

Provide a drinking place for butterflies by leaving out a
saucer of muddy water in a sunny corner of the garden.
This will give them the chance to sip on the water and take
in minerals that they may not source from nectar. Place some
pebbles in the saucer to weigh it down and provide a warm
landing place for the butterflies. Put some larger, smoother,
darker stones around the edge of the saucer, so the butterflies
can bask in the sun.

❧ BIRD OF THE MONTH ❧

Goldcrest

Europe's smallest bird, the goldcrest is still nesting in July,
raising its second brood. This busy, industrious bird is often
active near humans as it forages for spiders and tiny insects.
It is most likely to be seen feeding around coniferous
woodland, unmistakable because of its black crown, which
has a distinctive central yellow stripe.

❧ GARDEN EVENTS ❧

Hampton Court Garden Festival, 2–7 July
A flower show on a grand scale, with show gardens, floral marquees, rose exhibits and an enormous range of food, drink and craft outlets. This is a big summer day out for garden and plant lovers.

National BBQ Week
With long evenings and warm nights, early July is the time to make the most of your BBQ and host some alfresco dining in the garden, garnished with freshly picked salad and herbs.

National Preserving Awareness Week
Celebrate the art of preserving your own food this week. Fresh blackcurrants and gooseberries from the garden are a good place to start, whether making your own jams or freezing the fruits. A blackcurrant crumble in winter is a tangy, warming delight.

J

Visit a National Trust garden such as Beningbrough Hall, Yorkshire, to be inspired by their fruit garden, one of the first National Trust kitchen gardens to be renovated. Or head to Chartwell, Kent, to see their 1920s walled kitchen garden and resident chickens.

Big Butterfly Count
Download a butterfly ID chart or free app for your phone and record butterfly sightings in your garden to help Butterfly Conservation assess the health of our environment.

Outdoor Theatre

Watching a play on a balmy summer night in the beautiful ground of a National Trust estate is a fine way to celebrate summer and there will be a full programme of theatre, cinema and music to enjoy in the open air at many National Trust locations this July. Check their website for details of events near you.

Belvoir Castle Flower and Garden Show

Held within the estate of Belvoir Castle, enjoy the show borders created by designers taking part in The London College of Garden Design's competition. Also enjoy gardening demonstrations, sculpture artists, crafts and live music.

RHS Tatton Park Flower Show

The Floral Marquee exhibits a range of innovative show gardens full of planting ideas to try at home, which will keep your garden looking wonderful in late summer.

'There are always flowers for those who want to see them.'
– Henri Matisse

NATIONAL TRUST GARDENS
❧ AT THEIR BEST ❧
(with mazes)

Cliveden, Buckinghamshire
If you want to challenge the whole family, take on the maze at Cliveden, made up of more than a thousand 2m (6.6ft) high yew trees. Try not to get lost as you trek through 500m (1,640ft) of winding paths.

Lyveden, Northamptonshire
A great place for children to play hide and seek, the old labyrinth here has been cut into the grass to replicate the original pattern. In summer, wildflowers grow up around the edges of the paths.

Speke Hall, Merseyside
Designed by leading maze designer Adrian Fisher, the mysterious maze at Speke Hall has six routes, five bridges, twelve gates and a tower.

J

Glendurgan Garden, Cornwall
Originally built and conceived in 1833, the cherry laurel maze at Glendurgan sits on a slope, with 173 steps within the maze. There is a palm tree in each corner and a small, thatched pavilion in the centre.

Trivia
The maze at Glendurgan contains 650m (2,132ft) of paths and was installed by Alfred Fox. He would fine any cheating child who broke through the hedges the sum of one shilling.

Cragside, Northumberland

Known as Nelly's Labyrinth, the network of winding paths and tunnels cut out of a vast rhododendron forest is sure to delight children in need of some exercise and a challenge.

Trivia
Florence Court in County Fermanagh has a common lime (Tilia x europaea) with a girth of 10.78m (35.37ft) – the widest in the UK.

'Just living is not enough … one must have sunshine, freedom, and a little flower.'
– Hans Christian Andersen

YOUR NOTES FOR
❧ NEXT YEAR ❧

What has worked

_____

_____

_____

_____

_____

_____

What hasn't

_____

_____

_____

_____

_____

_____

What I'd like to try

_____

_____

_____

_____

_____

_____

_____

_____

J

Rudbeckia in flower

August

*'The English winter – ending in July,
to recommence in August.'*
– Lord Byron

August is the month when age starts to catch up with the garden. Lots of plants have had their heyday and the garden is more a place of burnished shades and faded glory, rather than polish and freshness. But it has a beauty of its own, a richness and depth that is to be celebrated as much as the youthfulness of spring. It's another busy month of harvesting beans, tomatoes, squashes and salad, as well as cutting back. Perhaps most importantly, it's the time for relentless deadheading in order to keep the garden as floriferous and colourful as possible. With late-flowering bulbs and perennials in the garden, it can be as colourful a month as any, even in a heatwave.

❧ SUNRISE AND SUNSET 2024 ❧

Location	Date	Rise	Set
Belfast			
	Aug 01 (Thu)	05:35 BST	21:24 BST
	Aug 11 (Sun)	05:53 BST	21:03 BST
	Aug 21 (Tue)	06:11 BST	20:41 BST
	Aug 31 (Sat)	06:30 BST	20:17 BST
Cardiff			
	Aug 01 (Thu)	05:37 BST	21:00 BST
	Aug 11 (Sun)	05:53 BST	20:42 BST
	Aug 21 (Tue)	06:08 BST	20:22 BST
	Aug 31 (Sat)	06:24 BST	20:00 BST
Edinburgh			
	Aug 01 (Thu)	05:18 BST	21:19 BST
	Aug 11 (Sun)	05:37 BST	20:57 BST
	Aug 21 (Tue)	05:57 BST	20:34 BST
	Aug 31 (Sat)	06:16 BST	20:08 BST
London			
	Aug 01 (Thu)	05:25 BST	20:49 BST
	Aug 11 (Sun)	05:41 BST	20:31 BST
	Aug 21 (Tue)	05:56 BST	20:10 BST
	Aug 31 (Sat)	06:12 BST	19:49 BST

A

❧ WEATHER CHARTS ❧

Averages 1991–2020

Location		
Belfast	Max temperature (°C)	19.40
	Min temperature (°C)	11.47
	Days of air frost (days)	0.00
	Sunshine (hours)	141.86
	Rainfall (mm)	84.95
	Days of rainfall ≥1 mm (days)	13.52
Cardiff	Max temperature (°C)	21.43
	Min temperature (°C)	12.92
	Days of air frost (days)	0.00
	Sunshine (hours)	185.30
	Rainfall (mm)	104.82
	Days of rainfall ≥1 mm (days)	12.40
Edinburgh	Max temperature (°C)	19.07
	Min temperature (°C)	11.51
	Days of air frost (days)	0.00
	Sunshine (hours)	159.97
	Rainfall (mm)	71.57
	Days of rainfall ≥1 mm (days)	10.37
London	Max temperature (°C)	22.26
	Min temperature (°C)	13.35
	Days of air frost (days)	0.00
	Sunshine (hours)	188.25
	Rainfall (mm)	67.65
	Days of rainfall ≥1 mm (days)	9.25

❧ TASKS ❧

Things to start

Spinach

A hardy, nutritious and versatile vegetable, spinach sown this
month can be harvested right through winter. The seeds are
easy to handle and quick to germinate when sown direct
into the soil in a sunny or partly-shaded spot. Use the corner
of a hoe to make a row 1.5cm (0.6in) deep, water the base,
let the water drain, then sprinkle the seeds along the row.
Cover with compost or fine soil and germination should
take place in a couple of weeks.

Spring cabbage

It's easy to think that the time to start off some 'heavyweight'
crops has gone in August, but spring cabbages can be planted
now, and if you're quick at the start of the month, you could
sow some in a greenhouse or in a propagator on a sunny
windowsill. Plant 20cm (7.8in) apart in rows spaced 40cm
(15in) apart, burying the spindly part of the stem so the plant
is well anchored. Avoid soil that has been heavily mulched
with compost or manure because it may be too acidic.

Things to finish

Sweetcorn

Pierce the surface of a sweetcorn kernel with your finger. If
the juice is a milky white colour, then you've got something
delicious to add to your summer spreads. The taste of
sweetcorn, freshly picked and plunged straight into boiling
water, is something of a statement: it's the season for large,
substantial crops, with many more on the way (which is

A

evident if you've planted marrows). Once you've finished harvesting, chop up all the old sweetcorn stalks and put them in the compost.

Summer raspberries
The last of the summer raspberries will be picked this month. As soon as you have harvested them all, it's time to cut out the canes that bore fruit. In their place are fresh, green, new canes that will provide fruit next year. The old-fruited canes are woodier and paler, so easy to tell apart from the new ones. Cut the old ones flush to ground level.

❧ SOMETHING TO PRUNE ❧

Rambling roses
Most rambling roses only flower once, so will benefit from a bit of a tidy-up this month. If there are still some attractive hips on the plant, then you may want to delay it. To keep them tidy, completely prune out some of the oldest stems at

the base. This will allow good air circulation and prevent the plant from becoming a higgledy-piggledy mess of congested, tangled growth. Make the initial cut at the base, but you may need to cut the stem a few times further up in order to pull out all the unwanted growth. Long sleeves and a thick, sturdy pair of gloves is recommended for this job. You can also cut back the stems that flowered this year, depending on the space available, then tie them to their supports. Finish by cutting out any damaged or diseased growth and shortening sideshoots by half.

❧ SOMETHING TO SAVOUR ❧

Perennials

August is the month when a whole new fleet of flowering perennials announce themselves for the first time. It's like having a new group of guests arriving at a party, just when the conversation is starting to dry up. Asters, dahlias, sedums, Japanese anemones and rudbeckias add a wonderful richness to the garden, to celebrate the final throes of the season. Autumn evenings coloured by late perennials, glowing in the pink-tinged light will be truly special.

A

Cucumber

I never tire of stepping out into the garden in August and cutting a fresh, sun-warmed outdoor cucumber such as 'Marketmore'. The flesh is so wonderfully soft and succulent that it feels just as at home in a fruit salad as it does in a savoury dish. Even if you only have room for a couple of plants, there should be regular pickings this month. Keep feeding them with high-potassium liquid plant food (such as comfrey food) through the month.

❧ THRIFTY PROJECT ❧

August can sometimes be a washout, but it can also be a ferocious month for heatwaves, making watering feel overwhelming, especially during hosepipe bans. Recycling water used indoors will really help. Bath and washing-up water (grey water) can be saved in containers to water plants and will be safe to pour on the soil if used within 24 hours. Keeping a washing-up basin in your sink will collect a surprising amount of water. Pour the contents into a watering can and water some plants with it at the end of the day. Prioritise any plants that have been planted in the last 12 months, as they will be more vulnerable than established plants when it comes to coping with heat stress. Avoid using grey water on edible crops.

Water butts are a fantastic weapon to have in your armoury during a drought. Connect them to a downpipe running off a shed or house roof so that you are capturing a higher volume of rainwater. If butts are almost full and more rain is forecast, empty as much of the collected water as you can into cans and buckets to make more space in them. Remember that blueberries, camellias, rhododendrons, carnivorous plants and orchids will grow much better when watered with rainwater, rather than tapwater. Tapwater is more palatable for lime-lovers such as brassicas.

HEAD GARDENER'S JOB
❧ OF THE MONTH ᵴ

Pruning wisteria at Nymans, West Sussex
Head Gardener – Joe Whelan

At Nymans, wisteria is an important part of our significant plant collection. Some of them are more than 120 years old. We take great care to preserve and encourage our wisteria plants, so that visitors can experience their stunning displays for many years to come.

Left unchecked, wisteria will happily ramble up and along other vegetation and structures. For the best displays, a little bit of pruning goes a long way. The key is to keep new growth in check, and encourage light to be able to reach the base of the stems, to help ripen the wood and encourage flower buds.

In summer, we cut back new, whippy, green growth to at least six leaves. This helps light get through and keeps our plants tidy. If you are still in the process of training the wisteria, it's helpful to tie in this new growth while it's still flexible, rather than prune it.

A

Restricting the amount of vegetative growth maximises the potential for flowers, and the result is one of the most exceptional displays we have in the garden. The fragrant pea-like flowers are proper showstoppers in late spring, and with the right amount of pruning, will smother the entire plant for weeks at a time.

❧ PLANTS OF THE MONTH ❧

Rose 'Lady of Shalott'

This rose will hardly stop flowering from the end of May until at least the end of October. Its tantalising buds are a warm, glowing blend of orange and red, and its well-scented blooms shine a bright, deep orange, fading to a rich yellow. One of the healthiest shrub roses, it can stay in full leaf until the end of winter. If only lightly pruned, it can be grown as a short climber. Height: 1.8m (6ft).

Rudbeckia 'Goldsturm'

This perennial pops up late in the border, hardly noticeable when spring is in full swing and summer begins. However, by early August it is pumping out custard-yellow parasols that can be relied upon to bring colour into the garden until well into September. The stems are very sturdy and good at shrugging off squally weather. Remember to give it a good soak in hot spells and grow it in soil that doesn't dry out too quickly. Height: 75cm (2ft 6in).

Helenium 'Red Shades'

Another late arrival to a garden border, *helenium* is a great plant to pair with rudbeckias, providing a rich, velvety contrast to their bright, solid flowers. The blooms get more intriguing as they age. Its older, sepia-toned hues still look grand in winter, especially when edged with frost. Good in a semi-shaded spot in soil that isn't quick to dry out. Height: 1m (40in).

❧ WILDLIFE TO LOOK FOR ❧

Swallows

Look to the skies towards the end of August and you may
start to see a gathering of swallows on roofs and powerlines.
This is a sure sign that summer is on the wane, as they
prepare for their long journey south in search of food.
Swallows are tiny birds, not much bigger than a matchbox,
and feed on airborne insects such as bluebottles and large
flies. As their food becomes scarce here, they begin their
6,000-mile trip to Southern Africa.

A

Painted lady

These unmissable orange, black and white butterflies can be found feeding on the flowerheads of thistles this month. These butterflies are hardcore travellers, with eggs laid in Africa, resulting in adult butterflies that fly over to Europe, before making the return trip south. One generation of this butterfly can clock up 5,000 air miles.

Toadlets

Young toads begin to emerge from ponds at this time of year to spend the rest of the summer out of the water. Compost heaps and untidy heaps of stone slabs are favourite sheltering spots, as are the bottoms of hedges. Placing some rocks and logs close to the edge of the pond will also give them a place to rest.

❧ HOW TO HELP WILDLIFE ❦

Creating a pond will greatly increase the biodiversity of your garden. If you don't have space to dig a pond, make one in a container instead. A sealed butler's sink or an old tin bath are ideal. Make sure you use something solid, watertight and frost-proof and position it in a well-lit place. Try placing bricks inside your container to stand plants on, to help test out different planting depths. You ideally want to fill the container with saved rainwater, if possible, to reduce the risk of algal growth. Stack some logs to just below the rim of the container, to act as stepping stones for wildlife to get in and out.

❧ BIRDS OF THE MONTH ❧

Sparrow

August is moulting season for birds. Many will be hiding away this month, low on energy and seeking shelter to escape from predators. If your garden is close to arable farmland, then you may well have the joy of watching sparrows feasting on grain crops as harvest time approaches. There is an abundance of food this month and none more so than in a freshly harvested field.

Black-headed gull

This inland gull may not enter your garden but there's a chance that you will hear this noisy bird while you're busy outside. Despite its name this bird has a white head for most of the year, and even when the colour darkens in summer, it is more chocolate brown than black. Its Latin species name of *'ridibundus'* means laughing, referring to the nature of its loud call.

A

❧ GARDEN EVENTS ❧

National Allotments Week, 5–11 August

Celebrate the important role that allotments play in our communities by getting involved in a local event at an allotment site near you.

Hyde Hall Flower Show, 7–11 August

Take a visit to pick up gardening advice from a wide range of expert plant growers, discover spectacular summer flower displays and enjoy talks and demonstrations in the Potting Shed Theatre.

Shrewsbury Flower Show, 9–10 August

A diverse show to enjoy during the school summer holidays, with a wide range of exciting floral arrangements, live music and demonstrations from expert gardeners and chefs.

Afternoon Tea Week, 12–18 August

There are hundreds of National Trust places to unwind with a pot of tea and some tasty treats, including the Squires Pantry at Felbrigg Hall, Norfolk, where you can sit in the courtyard with a refreshment and soak up the sun.

Great Comp Garden Show

Set in the beautiful garden at Great Comp, savour the summer show, featuring specialist nurseries, local artists and craftspeople. The Old Dairy Tearoom in the garden will be open throughout the show.

Southport Flower Show

There's summer holiday fun here for all the family with children's entertainment, arena shows, talk theatre, show gardens, a food village and a large amateur grower's competition that is open to everyone. Take along your best marrow or bunch of roses.

NATIONAL TRUST GARDENS
❧ AT THEIR BEST ❧
(for the school summer holidays)

Gibside, Tyne & Wear

There's lots to do for children with a lot of energy to burn at Gibside. Take a family-friendly circular walk and discover adventure highlights along the way, including a den-building area, a low ropes course and the Strawberry Castle play area.

Trivia
The gardens at Kingston Lacy, Dorset, contain 118 allotment plots.

Killerton, Devon

The gardens at Killerton are full of wide-open spaces, perfect for little ones in need of exercise! Paths in the garden are also buggy-friendly and older children will enjoy a climb to the top of the Clump, where they will find a den-building area to test their construction skills.

A

Mount Stewart, County Down

There is a natural play area at Mount Stewart themed around the journeys, adventures and creatures found in the book *The Magic Inkpot*, by Marchioness Londonderry and Lady Margaret Brock.

Trivia
The apple tree at Woolsthorpe Manor, Lincolnshire, is the place where, in 1665, Sir Isaac Newton later claimed that the 'notion of gravitation came to mind' after he watched an apple fall from its boughs.

Penrhyn Castle and Garden, Gwynedd

As well as having an adventure playground and lots of trails to explore, Penrhyn is a splendid place to take children for a picnic. There's wide, unfussy lawns with tremendous views of Conwy Bay and Eryri National Park.

Tyntesfield, Somerset

Look out for the enchanted treehouse in the woods at Tyntesfield, where there's a rope swing and lots of good places for a game of hide and seek. There's also a sculpture trail, and children can try their hand at brass rubbings.

The Gertrude Jekyll Garden, Lindisfarne

A garden of fragrant blooms and dots of colour, restored to the original vision of legendary horticulturist Gertrude Jekyll. Jekyll originally designed the garden on Holy Island in 1911, wanting it to be a 'riot of colour' all year round.

'I like generosity wherever I find it, whether in gardens or elsewhere. I hate to see things scrimp and scrubby. Even the smallest garden can be prodigal within its limitations.'
−Vita Sackville-West

YOUR NOTES FOR
∾ NEXT YEAR ∾

What has worked

What hasn't

What I'd like to try

A

Apples

September

'*My garden is my most beautiful masterpiece.*'
– Claude Monet

September is a month when breathing space returns to the garden. Everything seems to let out a contented sigh, as if to say that life has mellowed. Ethereal warm evenings, with the garden bathed in a beautiful soft light, are times to reflect and celebrate the winding down of another growing season. Many birds are heading south and summer crops are coming to their end. The arrival of autumn is a time to enjoy rather than mourn. There is lots to harvest, less of an urgent need to water thirsty plants and the borders are as full as they've ever been.

∻ SUNRISE AND SUNSET 2024 ∻

Location	Date	Rise	Set
Belfast			
	Sep 01 (Sun)	06:32 BST	20:14 BST
	Sep 11 (Wed)	06:50 BST	19:49 BST
	Sep 21 (Sat)	07:08 BST	19:24 BST
	Sep 30 (Mon)	07:25 BST	19:01 BST
Cardiff			
	Sep 01 (Sun)	06:26 BST	19:58 BST
	Sep 11 (Wed)	06:42 BST	19:35 BST
	Sep 21 (Sat)	06:58 BST	19:12 BST
	Sep 30 (Mon)	07:12 BST	18:52 BST
Edinburgh			
	Sep 01 (Sun)	05:18 BST	21:19 BST
	Sep 11 (Wed)	05:37 BST	20:57 BST
	Sep 21 (Sat)	05:57 BST	20:34 BST
	Sep 30 (Mon)	06:16 BST	20:08 BST
London			
	Sep 01 (Sun)	06:14 BST	19:47 BST
	Sep 11 (Wed)	06:30 BST	19:24 BST
	Sep 21 (Sat)	06:46 BST	19:01 BST
	Sep 30 (Mon)	07:01 BST	18:40 BST

S

❧ WEATHER CHARTS ❧

Averages 1991–2020

Location

Belfast	Max temperature (°C)	17.34
	Min temperature (°C)	9.64
	Days of air frost (days)	0.00
	Sunshine (hours)	112.03
	Rainfall (mm)	69.64
	Days of rainfall ≥1 mm (days)	11.63
Cardiff	Max temperature (°C)	19.10
	Min temperature (°C)	10.70
	Days of air frost (days)	0.00
	Sunshine (hours)	151.89
	Rainfall (mm)	86.31
	Days of rainfall ≥1 mm (days)	11.8
Edinburgh	Max temperature (°C)	16.88
	Min temperature (°C)	9.65
	Days of air frost (days)	0.03
	Sunshine (hours)	130.09
	Rainfall (mm)	54.92
	Days of rainfall ≥1 mm (days)	9.93
London	Max temperature (°C)	19.13
	Min temperature (°C)	11.12
	Days of air frost (days)	0.00
	Sunshine (hours)	145.48
	Rainfall (mm)	59.08
	Days of rainfall ≥1 mm (days)	8.97

❧ TASKS ❧

Things to start

Green manures

Green manures – such as grazing rye, mustard and winter field beans – can be sown directly into bare areas of soil on the veg patch. Sowing green manure is a bit like cleaning skirting boards in the house, one of those jobs that's so easy to put off, but well worth it once done. Just scatter the seed over level, weed-free areas of soil and rake it in. For beans, sow them in rows as if you were sowing a crop of broad beans in spring. Green manures will begin to cover the ground through autumn, helping to stop weeds from getting a foothold and reducing the risk of the soil becoming waterlogged and eroding, which can wash out nutrients. Green manures also do exactly what they say on the tin, keeping otherwise empty areas looking green through winter. Once spring arrives, chop down the foliage then use a spade to dig it into the soil, down to around 20cm (8in), then leave it for a couple of weeks before preparing the soil for sowing.

Overwintering onions

Hardy overwintering onions such as 'Senshyu Yellow' can be sown now, ideally in areas of soil that drain very well. Planting these little bulbs now is one of those jobs that you can be forgiven for feeling a bit smug about. Walking through the garden in the middle of winter and seeing perky rows of onion shoots standing proud is a real confidence booster; a reminder that the 'grow your own' year is firmly underway very early, with tangible results already.

S

If your soil is a bit heavy, spread some gritty compost – or compost mixed with grit – over the soil surface before planting. Onions don't like to be in soggy, cold soil for too long or the bulbs can rot. Space the bulbs 10cm (4in) apart and plant so the tips are only ever so slightly above the soil surface. Trim the tips with scissors if they are long, otherwise curious birds will enjoy pulling them out. Insert a large label at the end of the row until the bulbs start shooting. They will be ready to harvest as spring onions in April and as big onions in early summer.

Things to finish

Tomatoes

If tomatoes grown outside have managed to avoid blight up until now, it's time to gather what's left at the end of the month. Even if they are still green, they will ripen indoors if placed near some ripe bananas, or you could add them to chutneys, stews or salsas. Discard any fruits that carry the brown blotches that signal blight, and put the old plants in your garden waste recycling bin rather than on your compost heap. Clean the ground around the plants, removing all the old fruits and foliage, otherwise you may end up with a lot of unwanted tomato seedlings popping up next spring, which won't come true to type.

Potatoes

Foliage on potatoes still in the ground should turn yellow and start to wither this month, indicating that it's harvest time. Cut off the dying foliage a week or so before harvesting. Insert a digging fork away from the edge of the ridge where the potatoes were planted and lever it up to unearth them. Don't dig in too close to where the top growth was or there's a good chance that you'll skewer a few spuds. Ideally, lift potatoes on a dry, sunny day so you can leave the crop out to dry for a couple of hours. Store them in an unlit, unheated place (a garage or shed is ideal) in brown paper bags with the top rolled over to keep them dark. This stops the tubers going green.

❧ SOMETHING TO PRUNE ☙

Blackberries (and hybrid berries)

Here's a task that requires some protective clothing. The juicy fruits of blackberries (plus tayberries, boysenberries and loganberries) will have withered and the thorny stems that carried the fruit need cutting off the plant now their work is done. Afterwards, you'll be left with all the new growth, which will flower next year and can be tied in if necessary. Start off as far down on the plant as possible and use loppers to cut off the fruited stems. Hold the cut stem in between the cutting blades of the loppers and pull them until they are completely released from the plant. Sometimes you'll need to cut off a couple of sideshoots if the stem is getting tangled. Then chop the stems in half again so you have a neat pile that can be carried to the compost heap (thick gloves required). These stems are good for placing at the bottom of a new compost heap, or you can shred the stems and add them to a heap already underway. A few of the stems laid over bare soil are handy for deterring cats from using the area as a bathroom.

S

❧ SOMETHING TO SAVOUR ❧

Grasses in flower

September is the month when grasses start to make the transition from background supporters to garden stars. Many *Miscanthus*, stipe and *Pennisetum* are now showing off plumes of feathery flower stalks, adding something akin to nature's fireworks to the garden. Plant grasses on the east side of a garden, so that the low setting sun can make them sparkle even more. When mingled with the late flowers of roses, dahlias, salvias and rudbeckias, the end result is truly something to sit back and enjoy with an evening drink in the garden.

The first apples

The apple-picking season is really in full swing in October, but the earliest varieties such as 'Discovery' and 'Worcester Pearmain' should be ready to pick early this month. Few harvests are as memorable and satisfying as the first apples of the season. Perhaps because the fruits have been visible for so long, but the thought of picking is always something to be saved 'for later'. Then there's the tantalising 'twist test'. Apples are ready to pick when they fall from the tree after being given a gentle twist. It's hard to resist checking them every day, as soon as they look big enough for picking. It is also tempting to yank them off the tree early in anticipation. Leave them alone and it will be well worth the wait: a perfectly ripe apple from the garden is a wondrous thing.

❧ THRIFTY PROJECT ❦

Recycled seed trays for salad

If you regularly buy mushrooms from the supermarket, then you're also buying a seed tray at the same time. Mushroom containers are perfect for starting some windowsill salads that will keep you in nutritious fresh leaves for the whole of autumn with regular sowing (every one or two weeks). Use scissors to snip out a few drainage holes and place them on a tray (you can use an old ice cream tub lid rather than buying plant trays). Recycle some spent compost from crops in containers to half fill the trays, then just use fresh compost to fill the second half. Sow some mixed salad evenly across the compost after watering it, then cover with sieved compost, vermiculite or perlite.

S

HEAD GARDENER'S JOB
❧ OF THE MONTH ❧

Pruning yew hedges at Blickling Estate, Norfolk
Head Gardener – Ed Atkinson

No one forgets their first sight of Blickling, with the iconic red-brick Hall framed by 400-year-old yew hedges at the heart of the estate. With such a pivotal role in the history and experience of Blickling, it is essential that the yew hedges are maintained so they continue to flourish.

Stay sharp
Having super sharp blades to cut our yew is essential. Yew has a habit of tearing, especially when cut with a blunt blade, leaving unsightly white sappy strands.

A need for speed
If you use a powered hedge trimmer, buy the fastest reciprocating model available. Yews are known for their density of new stems and we use a fast machine to help cut through this.

Keep it clean
We use a leaf blade to help keep things tidy. This scoop-like attachment enables us to cut, gather and throw the loose material away from the hedge in one swift movement, making for a quick clean up afterwards.

Whether it has smooth curves, straight lines, or a perfectly level top, a well-cut yew hedge is a structural gem in any garden. At Blickling, they frame views, create a backdrop for floral displays and contribute to the ornamental display of the parterre, and it's all down to their careful shaping.

❧ PLANTS OF THE MONTH ❧

Abelia x grandiflora
This delightful shrub brings the freshness of spring to
late summer and early autumn. It is a perfectly poised
shrub, with small, super-glossy oval leaves on sturdy but
beautifully arching branches that hold clusters of delicately
scented, pale pink trumpet flowers. It needs a sunny, sheltered
spot and good drainage to make sure it gets through a hard
winter, although it should be hardy to -10°C (14°F).
Height: 3m (10ft).

Dahlia 'Art Deco'
Of all the thousands of dahlias available, everyone has their
favourites. What an incredible show they continue to put on
this month, seemingly oblivious that the days are becoming
shorter and plant growth is slowing down. 'Art Deco' is a
short form that is good for planting at the front of a border,
so that the many shades of pinkish red and pale orange
shown off by the wavy petals can be enjoyed to the max.
Height: 90cm (3ft).

Persicaria virginiana var. filiformis
This curious plant is reluctant to come to the party: sitting
in suspended motion for most of summer, with a small
clump of shield-shaped, chevroned leaves, never threatening
to be noticed. Then all of a sudden it's September and an
array of the unusual leaves have filled out to form a lush,
jungly clump, high and wide, and topped with the most
intriguing strands of miniscule maroon flowers, held on thin
red stems. Height and width: 60cm (2ft).

S

❧ WILDLIFE TO LOOK FOR ❧

Speckled bush cricket

Sit out in the garden on a quiet September evening and you may well be treated to the soundtrack of bush crickets chirping, the music made by the way the males rub their wings together. They are most active at dusk and common in areas of thick vegetation, so if you've left a bit of your lawn to go wild, you've got a good chance of them being in your garden.

Footballer hoverfly

The footballer hoverfly is given its nickname because of its distinctive black and yellow striping, resembling a footballer's kit (perhaps even more relevant if you support Watford F.C. or Borussia Dortmund). If you have the nectar-packed flowers of sedum (*Hylotelephium*), verbena, buddleja, and valerian in your garden, then you may well see this brightly coloured pollinator buzzing about.

Hawker dragonflies

If it stays mild, these large, late-flying dragonflies can be seen in gardens as late as November. Adult flies are up to 6cm (2in) long and will be busy looking for food (small flying insects) in grassy areas in your garden this month. They are something of a show-off, putting on their own aerial display in the garden, able to turn sharply, hover and fly backwards.

❧ HOW TO HELP WILDLIFE ❧

Plant some wallflowers this month to prepare the garden for the arrival of early-foraging insects next spring. Often sold cheaply in damp bare-root bundles in nurseries from now until late autumn, wallflowers are easy plants to grow in thin, well-drained soil in a sunny spot. Plant them deeply so any spindly stems are buried. Not only does their bushy habit keep the garden looking lush and full in winter, they will start to flower in early spring and provide a feast for early bees. They will also attract butterflies that have emerged from their winter sleep.

❧ BIRDS OF THE MONTH ❧

Whitethroat
These little warblers will begin their long journey to the Sahara soon, so are looking to stock up on berries to fuel their journey. They are rapid birds, with long tails; the males have white throats, while the females are off-white. See them underneath hedges and in rough areas of nettles and brambles.

S

Jay
Even though this is somewhat of an elusive garden bird that prefers to stay out of the limelight and remain in covered spots away from danger, you can't miss its rather painful, screeching call. More likely to be seen and heard in gardens with lots of mature trees, it is particularly fond of acorns. Its plumage is a dull pink and its wings black and white, but it's the exquisite blue and black chequered pattern at the front of its wing that it is most known for.

❧ GARDEN EVENTS ❧

Harrogate Autumn Flower Show, 13–15 September
A rich celebration of autumn with a wide range of autumn flowers from specialist nurseries, as well as the famous exhibition vegetables and the popular Heaviest Onion Competition.

Malvern Autumn Show, 27–29 September
Lots of autumn highlights are on show here, from giant vegetables to an RHS Floral Marquee, full of beautiful seasonal plants. Talks from expert gardeners and demonstrations in the cookery theatre make it a packed show.

National Organic Month
A celebration of organic food and drink encouraging shoppers and gardeners to try products that are free from potentially harmful chemicals.

Heritage Open Days Festival
A packed programme of special events and activities take place for England's largest festival of history and culture, with free opening for many of the Trust's most famous places.

Scottish Wild Food Festival
Take part in a festival encouraging people of all ages to step outdoors and learn about local wild food and foraging.

NATIONAL TRUST GARDENS
❧ AT THEIR BEST ❧
(by the sea)

Coleton Fishacre, Devon
Edged by coastal cliffs, this
delightful Devon garden is
the setting for a tranquil
walk that will have you
weaving through glades
and ponds, with tantalising
glimpses of the sea along
the way. The unique coastal
microclimate allows for
many exotic plants such
as cannas and bromeliads
to flourish.

Trivia
'Holy Corner' in the
gardens at Glendurgan
features plants from the
Bible, including olive trees
and a Judas tree (Cercis
siliquastrum).

Mottistone, Isle of Wight
This spectacular sheltered garden surrounds an Elizabethan
manor house, and is packed with exciting colours from an
array of tropical plants. See African grasses, tall ginger lilies
and double herbaceous borders packed with every colour
of flower imaginable.

Overbeck's Garden, Devon
A garden in the cliffs. Overlooking the breath-taking estuary
at Salcombe, Overbeck's garden wraps itself around the
seaside home of scientist and inventor Otto Overbeck. It's
a sub-tropical paradise with tall palm trees and formal beds
packed with colourful exotic plants.

S

Plas Newydd, Anglesey

With stunning views of Eryri National Park, the vast gardens at Plas Newydd are a coastal delight. The Italianate terrace is filled with flame-coloured plants, with cannas, rudbeckias and dahlias adding a fiery warmth to the end of summer and beginning of autumn. On a walk through the intriguing woodland you'll see Chilean beeches and eucalyptus.

Trivia
Some of the bricks in the walled garden at Chartwell, Kent, were laid between 1925 and 1932 by Sir Winston Churchill.

'There is no spot of ground, however arid, bare or ugly, that cannot be tamed into such a state as may give an impression of beauty and delight.'
– Gertrude Jekyll

YOUR NOTES FOR
❧ NEXT YEAR ❧

What has worked

_____
_____
_____
_____
_____

What hasn't

_____
_____
_____
_____
_____

What I'd like to try

_____
_____
_____
_____
_____
_____

S

Tawny owl

October

'Season of mists and mellow fruitfulness,
Close bosom-friend of the maturing sun;
Conspiring with him how to load and bless
With fruit the vines that round
the thatch-eves run.'
– John Keats

O

By the end of October, the garden has a very different feel to it than it does at the start. At the beginning of the month, there are tree fruits, squashes and autumn raspberries to pick, and late perennials are still holding their colour. By the end there is a real feeling that the growing season is over, with the abundance of autumn leaf colour now taking centre stage. Despite so many things coming to an end, it's also a month of new beginnings; every spring bulb planted is a beacon of hope and of brighter days to come.

❧ SUNRISE AND SUNSET 2024 ❧

Location	Date	Rise	Set
Belfast			
	Oct 01 (Tue)	07:27 BST	18:59 BST
	Oct 11 (Fri)	07:46 BST	18:34 BST
	Oct 21 (Mon)	08:05 BST	18:11 BST
	Oct 31 (Thu)	07:25 GMT	16:49 GMT
Cardiff			
	Oct 01 (Tue)	07:14 BST	18:49 BST
	Oct 11 (Fri)	07:31 BST	18:27 BST
	Oct 21 (Mon)	07:48 BST	18:06 BST
	Oct 31 (Thu)	07:05 GMT	16:47 GMT
Edinburgh			
	Oct 01 (Tue)	07:16 BST	18:47 BST
	Oct 11 (Fri)	07:37 BST	18:21 BST
	Oct 21 (Mon)	07:57 BST	17:56 BST
	Oct 31 (Thu)	07:18 GMT	16:34 GMT
London			
	Oct 01 (Tue)	07:02 BST	18:38 BST
	Oct 11 (Fri)	07:19 BST	18:15 BST
	Oct 21 (Mon)	07:36 BST	17:54 BST
	Oct 31 (Thu)	06:54 GMT	16:35 GMT

O

❧ WEATHER CHARTS ❧

Averages 1991–2020

Location

Belfast	Max temperature (°C)	13.80
	Min temperature (°C)	6.92
	Days of air frost (days)	0.60
	Sunshine (hours)	92.36
	Rainfall (mm)	95.83
	Days of rainfall ≥1 mm (days)	13.77
Cardiff	Max temperature (°C)	15.25
	Min temperature (°C)	7.99
	Days of air frost (days)	0.93
	Sunshine (hours)	103.87
	Rainfall (mm)	129.05
	Days of rainfall ≥1 mm (days)	15.03
Edinburgh	Max temperature (°C)	13.37
	Min temperature (°C)	6.72
	Days of air frost (days)	1.27
	Sunshine (hours)	99.35
	Rainfall (mm)	75.71
	Days of rainfall ≥1 mm (days)	11.73
London	Max temperature (°C)	14.83
	Min temperature (°C)	8.34
	Days of air frost (days)	0.33
	Sunshine (hours)	106.29
	Rainfall (mm)	78.57
	Days of rainfall ≥1 mm (days)	11.03

❧ TASKS ❦

Things to start

Daffodils

Tulips can wait until November, or even December, but daffodils are best planted now to give their roots time to establish well before spring. Plant each bulb at a depth equal to two or three times the height of the bulb, and plant in groups to make a big impact. They are a good flower for growing in scruffy, wild sections of the garden, such as in long grass or at the base of hedges and grassy banks. In borders, they can be a bit tricky, with the old foliage needing to stay intact until the end of spring, which can cause a bit of a nuisance and be a bit of an eyesore in a packed area of mixed planting.

Broad beans

You might feel a little crazy sowing a new vegetable directly into the soil at this time of year, with the months of cold and darkness ahead, but it's a heartening, defiant task to do. Walking past fat, new seedlings standing proud in a couple of months' time is something of a morale boost. Choose varieties recommended for autumn sowing, such as 'Luz de Otono' or 'The Sutton'. Sow them 5cm (2in) deep in staggered double rows spaced around 20cm (8in) apart, so the young plants can support each other. Insert canes at the end of each row and tie string tightly around them all when the plants are young, to help keep them upright.

O

Things to finish

Pumpkins
It's best to get pumpkins and all winter squashes harvested by the end of the month, before the risk of frost becomes greater. If you have a lot to harvest and intend to store them for a long time, harvest with at least 8cm (3in) of stalk intact, which will prolong the keeping time. Sit the harvested fruits in a greenhouse or on a sunny window ledge for a week for the skins to cure, further extending their shelf life.

Carrots
Although carrots can be covered with straw or fleece so they can be harvested throughout winter, it's best to dig them up now, especially if your soil is a bit on the heavy side. They can rot if they're in very wet conditions for long periods (which in winter, they usually are). Choose a reasonably dry day to lift your crop, as this will save a lot of laborious washing, as well as water. Push a fork vertically into the soil around 10cm (4in) from the foliage with one hand, and use the other to grab the leaves. Gently pull them up as you lever the fork from the ground. Leave the roots to dry on an unheated windowsill indoors for a couple of hours, then brush off the soil and store them in an unheated, well-ventilated room, ideally in trays of sand. If this isn't possible, prepare them as if you were going to cook them, then lay them out on a baking tray lined with greaseproof paper and freeze for a couple of hours. Put them into freezer bags and put them back in the freezer until you need them.

❧ SOMETHING TO PRUNE ❧

Birch trees

Young birch trees are a beautiful sight all year round, but especially in winter when their silhouettes can be enjoyed against a clear winter sky, without intrusion from other more showy plants. The white bark of birches such as *Betula utilis* var. *jacquemontii* is also a spectacular feature – an antidote to the masses of dull colours that can easily predominate the landscape at this time of year. The sap of birch trees bleed when pruned in summer so trim them now to improve their shape. Cut unwanted low branches right back to where they started from, using clean, sharp loppers or a small pruning saw. You can also cut out spindly growth that is making the tree's structure too complicated. Sometimes less is more.

O

❧ SOMETHING TO SAVOUR ❧

Japanese maples

These compact trees are ideal for small gardens. Many are fitting subjects for the patio and are tremendously underrated when it comes to talking about low-maintenance plants. They naturally form very attractive shapes and are not hungry feeders. They are also one of the most suitable trees to grow in pots because of their naturally spreading habits and slow growth. This is the month to marvel at them in a corner of dappled shade, where they thrive. 'Emerald Lace' is a riot of orange, red and purple, while 'Crimson Queen' adds some vivid scarlet as its leaves enter their final throes.

Exotic plants

This is the last month to enjoy the jungle generosity of exotic plants that aren't hardy, before they are wrapped for winter or pulled up and composted. Those grown as annuals such as *Ricinus communis* (castor oil plant), gazanias, morning glory and *Amaranthus* have filled an enormous amount of space and their wild and unmissable colours will still be evident for at least the first half of the month. Banana and tree ferns will be at their largest, luscious and leafy, so bask in their abundance before it's time to say goodbye. Be sure to take lots of pictures of them, because no two years in the garden are ever the same.

❧ THRIFTY PROJECT ❧

Maintaining tools

If you've invested in good quality tools, then make sure to invest some time in good quality maintenance. Keep them working well and you'll eliminate the need to buy anything else. There's nothing like a sharp pair of secateurs to make gardening easier and less strenuous – and will also mean healthier plants. Take secateurs and loppers apart and spray all the parts with WD-40, clean them using soapy water and a wire brush, and then dry them using an old rag. If blades are blunt or notched, use a handheld diamond tool sharpener to tune them up. Hold the angled side of the blade and apply pressure on it with the sharpener. Use a metal file to remove any burr to leave a nice clean edge. You'll be looking for excuses to snip something!

> *'Winter is an etching, spring a*
> *watercolour, summer an oil painting*
> *and autumn a mosaic of them all.'*
> – Stanley Horowitz

O

HEAD GARDENER'S JOB
❧ OF THE MONTH ❧

**Planting spring bulbs at Mount Stewart, County Down
Head Gardener – Mike Buffin**

Mount Stewart has a long tradition of spring bulb planting in the garden, as Edith, Lady Londonderry, filled the garden with her favourite spring bulbs including snowdrops, daffodils and tulips. The garden was especially renowned at 'tulip time' when her bulb season reached a crescendo in April and early May.

1. Always buy your bulbs from a reputable bulb supplier or garden centre. We have to check the bulbs are not rotten or shrivelled before planting.

2. We use a trowel to make the planting holes when planting in a border but if naturalising them below trees or in a lawn then use a bulb planter.

3. We plant our bulbs at a depth of two to three times greater than the depth of the bulb. Plant them pointy side up, hairy side down!

4. For the best effect for naturalising in lawns, we plant the bulbs randomly, whereas in borders and pots they can be more regimented and planted closer together.

Planting spring bulbs can enhance the colour of any garden and extend the season. The bulb season can start in January with snowdrops and daffodils and still be going in mid-May with the last flurry of tulips. Also try succession planting in terracotta pots using different types and colours of bulbs, which can be placed in areas as they flower.

❧ PLANTS OF THE MONTH ❧

Aster 'Kylie'

This unassuming hardy perennial gradually makes a well-branched, small-leaved bush, reaching about 60cm (2ft) tall if it is well-staked in spring. You will hardly notice it for five months until its cheery, pink daisy-flowers burst out in abundance this month, still showering the garden with bright blooms into November. It's hard not to stare at this plant in full bloom and think, 'Why didn't you arrive earlier?' But a far better question to ask is: what other late bloomers and evergreens can I plant around this autumn gem, to give October a fresher feel? A wispy stipa planted behind it will create something easy and ethereal. Height: 60cm (2ft).

Liriope muscari

Another tremendous plant for bringing autumn colour to a shady area, this exotic-looking lily is an evergreen perennial that will tolerate drought well. For a plant that can cope with challenging conditions, you might not expect it to look particularly exciting, but its spikes of bobbly purple flowers will add a dramatic twist to a border and can still show good colour next month too. Height: 30cm (12in).

O

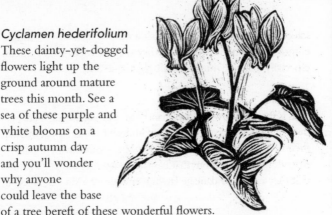

Cyclamen hederifolium
These dainty-yet-dogged
flowers light up the
ground around mature
trees this month. See a
sea of these purple and
white blooms on a
crisp autumn day
and you'll wonder
why anyone
could leave the base
of a tree bereft of these wonderful flowers.
Once the blooms are gone, the ground is decorated with
the unique, ornate leaves that follow after the flowers. This
perennial will self-seed easily and grows best in dappled
shade. Height: 10cm (4in).

❧ WILDLIFE TO LOOK FOR ❧

Ladybirds
Ladybirds may start looking for hibernating spots this
month, especially if the weather starts to turn cold. They are
seeking out warm, sheltered places to spend winter, so don't
be surprised if they start appearing indoors. If you've got a
lot of ladybirds in the house, tempt them into a jam jar and
tip them out in a warm spot under a hedge or in a sheltered
corner by a pile of dry leaves or twigs.

Tawny owls
Tawny owls may be heard this month, as those that fledged
in spring are out searching for a new home. This can lead
to 'arguments' with other owls so listen out for hoots and

screeches as competing owls thrash it out for territory. Although commonly found in woodland, they may visit suburban gardens, especially if tree cavities are available for nesting.

Badgers

This is the month when the chances of spotting a badger are at their highest. Badgers leave the sett at dusk to find food, doubling their body weight in order to survive the coming winter. They may visit feeding stations that contain peanuts, but keep in mind that they can badly damage lawns if encouraged into the garden.

❧ HOW TO HELP WILDLIFE ❧

Hedgehog house

Hedgehogs will be preparing for their winter hibernation, looking for a suitable dry place to spend the cold months ahead. A simple wooden house filled with dry leaves and placed in a sheltered corner of the garden has a good chance of being used by a hedgehog. Making one can also use up otherwise unwanted wooden offcuts that may be cluttering up the shed. A wooden crate is ideal. First, make an entrance hole, roughly 15cm (6in) square, in the side of the crate with a jigsaw. Then, create a simple entrance tunnel, around 30cm (12in) long, with wooden planks nailed together and into the side of the crate over the entrance hole. Nail down a wooden lid, completely covering the top of the crate.

❧ BIRDS OF THE MONTH ❧

Long-tailed tit

These tiny birds, with their distinctive high-pitched calls, are easily identified by their rounded bodies and long, slender tails. They prefer bushy woodland undergrowth, and are likely to be frequent visitors to bird feeders as the weather turns colder. Long-tailed tits are rather partial to suet blocks and fat balls to help them build up their fat reserves for winter.

Nuthatch

A small but portly bird, showing a beautiful contrast between its bluey grey plumage and its chestnut underwings. It also has distinctive black eye stripes, with white beneath. Feeding on nuts, seeds, beetles and spiders, it uses its sturdy beak to hide away its food in the crevices of tree trunks. Nuthatches aren't found in Ireland, but are increasing their spread further south.

❧ GARDEN EVENTS ❦

Seed Gathering Sunday, 13 October
Organised by the Tree Council, it's a day to collect tree seeds and start growing the trees of the future.

Apple Day, 21 October
A celebration of the vast number of different apples grown in the UK. Pay a visit to gardens with orchards to get involved – it's a great chance to broaden your horizons and get a taste for something different to the classic 'Braeburn' or 'Granny Smith'.

October Half Term
As well as enjoying the spectacular autumn colours, look out for great half-term events, from autumn wildlife spotting at Sutton Hoo, Suffolk, to an autumn colour hunt at The Vyne, Hampshire.

NATIONAL TRUST GARDENS
❧ AT THEIR BEST ❧
(for apples)

Beningbrough Hall, Yorkshire

The walled garden has an historic pear arch and is home to more than 90 different varieties of fruit, with 170 fruit trees and shrubs in the garden. The walls were first built in 1792 and enclose two acres of kitchen garden.

Brockhampton, Herefordshire

The gardens at Brockhampton contain five interlocking orchard 'rooms' which mimic the five seed chambers visible when an apple is cut open horizontally. The circular rooms have been planted to tell the story of how apple trees arrived in the UK and include rare and unusual trees.

> **Trivia**
> The Loggia (roofed walkway) in the gardens at Horton Court is believed to be the only one of its kind in the UK. It was built in the 1520s by William Knight, one of the lawyers leading divorce proceedings for Henry VIII.

Barrington Court, Somerset

There are ten acres of orchard to explore on the estate here, consisting of the Front Orchard, Goose Orchard and East Orchard. Most of the trees are cider apple varieties, with the bumper harvest – which is spread over a picking time of 12 weeks – used to make cider and apple juice.

Cotehele, Cornwall

The Mother Orchard at Cotehele contains more than 300 trees, with 125 different varieties of apple to see. These include rarities such as 'Cornish Honeypinnick', 'Limberlimb', 'Pig's Nose' and 'Lemon Pippin'. The varieties chosen have been bred to survive the mild, damp climate of the south-west coast.

Acorn Bank, Cumbria

As well as having the largest herb garden of all National Trust gardens – home to more than 275 different types of herb – there is also a large orchard made up of more than 100 local apple varieties, and at the top of the orchard are four beehives.

'Planting ground is painting a landscape with living things.'
– Gertrude Jekyll

YOUR NOTES FOR
❧ NEXT YEAR ❦

What has worked

What hasn't

What I'd like to try

O

Rowan berries

November

'*Fall, leaves, fall; die, flowers, away;*
Lengthen night and shorten day.'
– Emily Brontë

Let's be honest, November can be a pretty sticky month, and not just underfoot. Crisp layers of autumn leaves turn to a trampled soggy layer of mud, plucky perennials that put on a summery show in October are now somewhat sorry-looking stems, and there's probably no sign of a hoar frost to make it all look pretty. Taking time to go and see autumn colour on some spectacular trees is the perfect pick-me-up though, and definitely worth making a special trip to some local tree hotspots. Busying yourself planting spring bulbs, garlic and onions is another good antidote to the feeling of growing season ending, as is gathering as many leaves as you can to make nutritious leaf mould. Think of these jobs as wise investments in a tricky time. You'll be glad you made the effort.

❧ SUNRISE AND SUNSET 2024 ❧

Location	Date	Rise	Set
Belfast			
	Nov 01 (Fri)	07:27 GMT	16:47 GMT
	Nov 11 (Mon)	07:47 GMT	16:28 GMT
	Nov 21 (Thu)	08:06 GMT	16:13 GMT
	Nov 30 (Sat)	08:22 GMT	16:03 GMT
Cardiff			
	Nov 01 (Fri)	07:07 GMT	16:45 GMT
	Nov 11 (Mon)	07:25 GMT	16:28 GMT
	Nov 21 (Thu)	07:41 GMT	16:16 GMT
	Nov 30 (Sat)	07:55 GMT	16:08 GMT
Edinburgh			
	Nov 01 (Fri)	07:20 GMT	16:31 GMT
	Nov 11 (Mon)	07:42 GMT	16:11 GMT
	Nov 21 (Thu)	08:02 GMT	15:55 GMT
	Nov 30 (Sat)	08:18 GMT	15:45 GMT
London			
	Nov 01 (Fri)	06:56 GMT	16:33 GMT
	Nov 11 (Mon)	07:13 GMT	16:16 GMT
	Nov 21 (Thu)	07:30 GMT	16:03 GMT
	Nov 30 (Sat)	07:44 GMT	15:55 GMT

N

❧ WEATHER CHARTS ❧

Averages 1991–2020

Location		
Belfast	Max temperature (°C)	10.67
	Min temperature (°C)	4.18
	Days of air frost (days)	3.74
	Sunshine (hours)	52.87
	Rainfall (mm)	102.34
	Days of rainfall ≥1 mm (days)	15.52
Cardiff	Max temperature (°C)	11.61
	Min temperature (°C)	4.87
	Days of air frost (days)	3.66
	Sunshine (hours)	65.02
	Rainfall (mm)	130.65
	Days of rainfall ≥1 mm (days)	15.60
Edinburgh	Max temperature (°C)	9.86
	Min temperature (°C)	3.77
	Days of air frost (days)	5.27
	Sunshine (hours)	72.13
	Rainfall (mm)	65.25
	Days of rainfall ≥1 mm (days)	11.70
London	Max temperature (°C)	10.60
	Min temperature (°C)	5.04
	Days of air frost (days)	2.41
	Sunshine (hours)	67.19
	Rainfall (mm)	75.71
	Days of rainfall ≥1 mm (days)	11.93

❧ TASKS ❧

Things to start

New hedges

The bare-root season begins in November. This is when some plants are sold without pots but lifted from a field, with their roots bare. It's strange that this has become an unusual thing, as before the advent of garden centres, it was the main way that plants were bought: direct from the nursery. If you want to plant a new hedge, bare-root is the best way. Lots of plants can be easily posed in bundles tied together – no plastic needed – and are freshly lifted from a field, without any of the growing stress involved with pots and compost. Plant immediately into weed-free soil, at a distance of around 45cm (18in) between each plant, or a little closer if you're looking to quickly create a thick hedge. You should be able to see a point near the base of the stem where the colour changes slightly. This indicates how deeply the plant was planted in the field, so plant it at the same depth.

Soft fruit patches

Now is a good time to reflect on which crops you would like more of next year and, in my opinion, you can never have enough soft fruits. Bare-root currants and berries are available now, and garden centres are often discounting potted plants at this time of year. A few minutes planting this month can massively pay off as early as next summer, with an increase in fresh fruit from the garden. Choose a sunny spot for some new additions and keep it simple. If a particular type of fruit is thriving in one spot in the garden, add more as close to them as possible. If you're running out of space, currants, gooseberries and blueberries will all grow well in containers.

N

Things to finish

Swedes
Fewer crops possess such a vast chasm between how appetising they look and how delicious they are on the table. Mashed swede with a twist of black pepper is one of the most delicious things from the garden in late autumn and winter. The roots should easily pull up now and are best kept in a cold, unheated place indoors. If your soil is free-draining you can leave them in the soil to harvest when needed.

Autumn raspberries
The last of these seemingly relentless soft fruits will have been picked early this month – their sweetness gradually diminishing over the weeks. In many ways it serves as a stark reminder that the garden is entering a new phase. Further crops to come in the next couple of months are not on the soft and sweet side, and it will be many months until there is any fresh fruit to eat. Therefore, make the most of every last mouthful to mark the end of another growing season.

❧ SOMETHING TO PRUNE ❧

Roses
Bush roses can be very 'leggy' at this time of year. It's not unusual for some to send up shoots that far exceed the height that is given on the label. Long shoots of growth made this year will be heavy now, and can unsettle the roots of the plant as strong autumn gales blow through. Now is a good time to cut them down by half to keep the plant settled, to remove the old foliage, and to stop any infected leaves spoiling new growth early next year. Strip all the old leaves off the stems that remain after pruning.

❧ SOMETHING TO SAVOUR ❧

Beautiful berries

This is the time to enjoy the brightly coloured display of
fruits on shrubs and in hedgerows, before the weather turns
cold and they attract the attention of foraging birds. Hollies,
spindle (*Euonymus europaeus*), hawthorn, rowans and dog
roses are resplendent in November and our gardens are
poorer without them, both for the colour and richness they
bring through late autumn and winter, and for the valuable
food source they provide to garden birds.

N

The structure of the garden

As a lot of plants start to fade and leaves begin to drop, elements of the garden that provide the 'backbone' such as evergreen trees, shrubs and hedges, or trees with eye-catching 'skeletons' and bark start to come to the fore. The ageing stems and mature seedheads of tall, sturdy perennials will also start to stand out, and by the end of the month it will dawn on you that these will be your companions through winter. Prized statues give the garden permanence and allow hoar frosts to decorate them so superbly in the weeks to come.

❧ THRIFTY PROJECT ❧

Now is a great opportunity to visit garden centres and nurseries to take advantage of plants that are being reduced in price. These reductions are often because plants are looking a bit tatty but typically not because there is anything majorly wrong with them. Consider each reduced plant that takes your eye, and compare them to similar-looking plants in the garden now. Also check if the plant is hardy, because some sellers – often not specialists – will try and sell plants that are soon to be killed by frost and won't return. A tatty-looking perennial that has naturally died down is the perfect plant to snap up at a lower cost than usual. If shrubs are reduced, it might be that the plant has spent too long in its small pot and just needs more time in the garden soil.

HEAD GARDENER'S JOB
❧ OF THE MONTH ❦

Pruning climbing roses at Powis Castle, Powys
Head Gardener – David Swanton

There are lots of climbing roses planted throughout the garden at Powis Castle, and the varieties chosen have colours that blend in with the surrounding planting. They grow on the terrace walls, on pillars, and we grow them around poles in the formal garden.

November is a good time to prune climbing roses because the stems are still flexible this month. This allows them to be teased out if stems have grown behind their supports and they can be easily trained and tied to where we want them to grow.

To prune, we remove one or two of the oldest stems at the base of the plant and cut out any stems that are crossing into others, and those that are dead or damaged. We then bend the remaining stems at an angle of 45 degrees and cut the sideshoots back to two or three buds from the base of the shoot. These stems are then tied in with brand new ties. We also remove all the old leaves from the plant, both those on the plant and those on the ground at the base, to reduce the risk of fungal disease.

The bare pruned roses are a work of art in themselves at the start of the year and popular with visitors. From early summer, the result of the pruning and training sees a plant that is covered from top to bottom in flowers, creating pillars of colour.

N

❧ PLANTS OF THE MONTH ❧

Carex 'Everillo'

This evergreen sedge is a tremendous plant, both for adding strong autumn and winter colour to the garden and for being frosted – when its spidery, spreading strands positively sparkle as their luminous shades are brightened by a low sun. It's a real gift to the patio right now, superb for finishing off container displays by decorating the edges with its gently arching foliage. Grow in any soil except waterlogged soil, in full sun or part shade. Grow in very well-drained soil if you garden in the north, or a wet winter may see it perish. Height: 40cm (15in).

Miscanthus 'Ferner Osten'

This is a superb plant for planting at the back of a border to help knit other plants together and show them off. Its rich foliage shows shades of copper and brownish-red and the feathery plumes, which start out dark red, provide a neat, unassuming backdrop for bright greens and late autumn flowers. It will become one of your star plants in frosty conditions. Grow in full sun in any soil except waterlogged soil. Height: 1.6m (5ft 4in).

Imperata cylindrica 'Rubra'

Known as the Japanese blood grass, this perennial shows off blood red, bolt upright foliage at the start of autumn, before changing to crimson then brown as the season progresses. Growing to around 45cm (18in) tall it is a wonderful plant for squeezing into gaps at the front of a summer border to give it a late flourish of intense colour. Grow in full sun in moist, fertile soil that is slow to dry out. Height: 45cm (18in).

❧ WILDLIFE TO LOOK FOR ❦

Harvestman
Often mistaken for spiders, harvestmen actually belong to another group of arachnids called Opilones. In the garden, they are most likely to be discovered in leaf litter or in grass. They don't spin webs but they have hooks at the end of their legs, which they use to trap small invertebrates.

Hazel dormouse
This tiny mammal – no more than 9cm (3.5in) long and weighing about the same as a packet of crisps – will be feasting on nuts, seeds and berries to build up its fat reserves to survive winter. As the weather turns cold, they will leave their nests in tree branches and head for the ground. Here, they will build a tiny nest about the size of a tennis ball, out of grass and leaves.

Red-green carpet moth

This pretty moth has green wings flecked with streaks or patches of red and will still be taking flight this month before hibernating. Only the females hibernate, with mating occurring in autumn, and females laying eggs in spring; males do not survive winter. Look out for these moths on the wing if you trigger an outdoors security light on a mild night.

Comma butterfly

This orange and brown butterfly gets its name from the white spots beneath its wings, which are shaped like a comma. Having several broods a year and overwintering as adults, these butterflies are on the wing all year round and this month there's a good chance that you will find them feeding on fallen fruits. Their ragged-edged wings act as a useful camouflage, resembling fallen autumn leaves.

'If a tree dies, plant another in its place.'
– Carl Linnaeus

❧ HOW TO HELP WILDLIFE ❧

Leave seedheads intact

While summer and early autumn are a time of rigorous deadheading, November is the time to be less 'trigger happy' with your secateurs. It's very tempting to 'tidy up' and cut all the fading flower spikes and seedheads from plants that have finished flowering, but they have a lot to offer if left intact. As well as adding winter structure to the garden, seedheads prove valuable food for birds, both those that eat the seeds and those that eat the insects that congregate on the seedheads. Seedheads of sedum, teasel, echinacea and *Eupatorium maculatum* will attract birds this month.

❧ BIRD OF THE MONTH ❧

Starling

While some starlings are UK residents, others migrate from northern Europe to spend the winter here. Close-knit flocks of these noisy birds – twisting and turning as they fly together – will start building up this month, reaching a peak in January or February. Similar in size to a thrush, they are regular visitors to bird feeders and, as the season progresses, they are noticeable for a distinct buff spotting that develops on their feathers. Early evening is the best time to spot them.

N

❧ GARDEN EVENTS ❧

Guy Fawkes Night, 5 November
Coughton Court, Warwickshire, is the ideal place to find
out more about the notorious Gunpowder Plot. Ringleader,
Robert Catesby was the son of Sir William Catesby and
Anne Throckmorton of Coughton Court. Find out more
by paying a visit and let a National Trust volunteer tell you
the story.

Remembrance Sunday, 10 November
The world famous Sandham Memorial Chapel is open
along with The Garden of Reflection, planted by the Trust
in 2014 to mark the centenary of the commencement of
the First World War.

National Tree Week, 25 November–3 December
A nationwide event to celebrate the beginning of the tree
planting season and to acknowledge the role that trees and
woodland play in our lives. Events throughout the country
include talks, tree dressing and, of course, tree planting.

Cotehele Christmas Garland
This month, a team of volunteers begin to construct a
spectacular 18m (59ft) long flower garland to hang in the
great hall at Cotehele, Cornwall. It has been a tradition since
1956 for the gardeners at Cotehele to make a giant garland,
with flowers grown on the estate dried over the previous
summer. It takes ten days to construct and is typically made
up of in excess of 20,000 flowers.

NATIONAL TRUST GARDENS
❧ AT THEIR BEST ❧
(for autumn colour)

Sheringham Park, Norfolk

Full of remarkable trees, including veteran beeches and oaks
and golden larch (*Pseudolarix amabilis*), this is a spacious place
to enjoy large-scale autumn colour, and the park is also
home to around 100 species of fungi, including unusual lilac
mushrooms and golden bootlegs.

Hinton Ampner, Hampshire

With spectacular views of the
South Downs, a walk through the
grounds of Hinton Ampner this
month is spectacular as towering
oak, beech, chestnut and lime
trees dominate the landscape, and
Norway maples offer an autumn
leaf show in rich purple.

Trivia
*The oldest stumpery
in the UK is at
Biddulph Grange,
dating back to the
1850s.*

Stourhead, Wiltshire

The picturesque lake and architecture at Stourhead, with
grottoes, temples and bridges, is given the 'icing on the cake'
treatment as the mature woodland that surrounds the garden
glows with intricate autumn colours, reflected in the water.
A special place to stop and soak up the atmosphere, as well
as take pictures by the Pantheon or the Palladian Bridge.
With more than 2,500 acres of countryside to explore,
including walks through chalk downs and ancient woods,
perhaps the highlight is King Alfred's Tower, a 48.7m (160ft)
folly that offers panoramic views across three counties
(Wiltshire, Dorset and Somerset).

N

Wallington, Northumberland

The vast 13,500-acre estate at Wallington is a tremendous place to soak up some welcome autumnal sunshine. The East Wood is a must-visit spot in autumn, to see maple trees in all their multi-coloured autumn glory.

Sheffield Park, Sussex

A simply glorious place to be as autumn colours reach their peak. Vast maples, conifers and grasses light up the landscape and the lakes reflect the kaleidoscope of bold and beautiful leaf colours.

Winkworth Arboretum, Surrey

There are few better places to take a walk in autumn than among the 6,000 trees that make up this arboretum, originally the vast tree collection of Dr Wilfrid Fox.

> *'I do not enjoy planning when I am frozen to the marrow.'*
> – Beth Chatto

YOUR NOTES FOR
NEXT YEAR

What has worked

What hasn't

What I'd like to try

N

Robin

December

'Huge parsnips are difficult to dig up
and peeling them is like painting
the Forth Bridge.'
– Anna Pavord

D

December is perhaps an easier time to be a gardener than it should be, with so many Christmas traditions that go hand-in-hand with gardening. Brussels sprouts and parsnips can be harvested from the garden and eaten fresh on Christmas Day, and many gardens will be ripe grounds for the cutting of plant material for festive decorations. It is also a month when evergreens start to be appreciated again, as lots of perennials get flattened by wind and rain (or very occasionally snow), leaving you either marvelling at what wonderful structure your garden has, or determined to add more plants that hold their leaves all year. Often one of the soggiest months of the year, this may well be the time when you start taking more of an interest in houseplants until spring gets a bit closer.

❧ SUNRISE AND SUNSET 2024 ❧

Location	Date	Rise	Set
Belfast			
	Dec 01 (Sun)	08:23 GMT	16:02 GMT
	Dec 11 (Wed)	08:37 GMT	15:58 GMT
	Dec 21 (Sat)	08:45 GMT	16:00 GMT
	Dec 31 (Tue)	08:36 GMT	16:08 GMT
Cardiff			
	Dec 01 (Sun)	07:57 GMT	16:07 GMT
	Dec 11 (Wed)	08:08 GMT	16:04 GMT
	Dec 21 (Sat)	08:16 GMT	16:06 GMT
	Dec 31 (Tue)	08:18 GMT	16:14 GMT
Edinburgh			
	Dec 01 (Sun)	08:20 GMT	15:44 GMT
	Dec 11 (Wed)	08:34 GMT	15:38 GMT
	Dec 21 (Sat)	08:42 GMT	15:40 GMT
	Dec 31 (Tue)	08:44 GMT	15:49 GMT
London			
	Dec 01 (Sun)	07:45 GMT	15:55 GMT
	Dec 11 (Wed)	07:57 GMT	15:51 GMT
	Dec 21 (Sat)	08:05 GMT	15:54 GMT
	Dec 31 (Tue)	08:07 GMT	16:01 GMT

D

❧ WEATHER CHARTS ❧

Averages 1991–2020

Location

Belfast	Max temperature (°C)	8.44
	Min temperature (°C)	2.26
	Days of air frost (days)	7.07
	Sunshine (hours)	35.31
	Rainfall (mm)	93.25
	Days of rainfall ≥1 mm (days)	14.83
Cardiff	Max temperature (°C)	9.06
	Min temperature (°C)	2.84
	Days of air frost (days)	7.95
	Sunshine (hours)	50.44
	Rainfall (mm)	139.58
	Days of rainfall ≥1 mm (days)	15.17
Edinburgh	Max temperature (°C)	7.34
	Min temperature (°C)	1.57
	Days of air frost (days)	10.4
	Sunshine (hours)	49.15
	Rainfall (mm)	67.43
	Days of rainfall ≥1 mm (days)	12.30
London	Max temperature (°C)	7.81
	Min temperature (°C)	2.71
	Days of air frost (days)	7.74
	Sunshine (hours)	54.01
	Rainfall (mm)	68.25
	Days of rainfall ≥1 mm (days)	11.86

❧ TASKS ❧

Things to start

Onions from seed

Boxing day (26th December) was traditionally the day that exhibition growers started sowing onion seeds, in order to try and grow giant onions for flower shows. Even if you're not one for competitive growing, there's something defiant about taking a trip to the shed to start off a crop while everyone else is dozing off in front of the telly, arguing with relatives about the correct rules of Monopoly, or battling indigestion. Thinly sow the seeds in module trays, on the surface of some damp compost, then cover with vermiculite and keep at a temperature of 10–15°C (50–59°F).

Poinsettia

It's strange that such a commonly gifted houseplant at this time of year should also be quite a tricky one to grow. Perhaps a new trend for giving people cacti as presents needs to be launched? Anyway, if you end up with one of these curious plants place them away from radiators and cold draughts. Give them bright, indirect light and ideally keep them at a temperature of 15°C (59°F). Water sparingly each time the compost dries out.

Things to finish

Kale

December is the month to harvest the crown of kale plants, which will encourage sideshoots to form, ready to pick as a bonus harvest in February and March. It is best not to delay

D

picking, but to pick leaves little and often, to prevent them from becoming large, tough and too bitter for eating.

Purple sprouting broccoli

Sown in early spring, these hardy brassicas – hardy down to at least -10°C (50°F) – will be ready to gather this month. Harvest the shoots when they are strong, with well-developed flower buds that are yet to open. Cut the main spear in the centre of the plant, then the sideshoots will be ready later in winter or early spring.

❧ SOMETHING TO PRUNE ❧

Gooseberries

Pruning gooseberries each year makes them more productive, allows for easier picking and prevents them from taking up too much space. It's a high value task relative to the short amount of time spent doing it. Snip off any stems that are very close to ground level, as the fruits on this will spoil if they come into contact with the soil. Snip back all the sideshoots on the plant, pruning them to three buds from the base of the sideshoot, to encourage more fruits. Then shorten the ends of each main stem, cutting them back by around a third, to keep the plant neat and compact. Overly long stems can break easily.

❧ SOMETHING TO SAVOUR ❧

Visiting birds
As the weather turns colder, birds are more likely to visit feeders, as food becomes more scarce and they look to bolster their fat reserves to sustain them through the winter. Looking out into the garden and watching the birds visit your tables, feeders and suet blocks is a great spectator sport, especially if the weather doesn't allow for any gardening to be done. Sparrows and finches are fond of seeds, blue tits like fatty foods, and thrushes go for worms and fruits.

Colourful winter stems
The bright stems of *Rubus cockburnianus*, Cornus 'Midwinter Fire' and *Salix alba* 'Golden Ness' start to shine in the garden this month as all their foliage fades and their winter sculptures can be admired without any obstruction. They are a real pick-me-up on dull days, and December usually has its fair share of them. If you have plants with winter stems in pots, position them so that they can be easily viewed from the house.

D

❧ THRIFTY PROJECT ❧

Home-made decorations
A little bit of greenery cut from the garden can form the backbone of some simple, effective and unique seasonal decorations. Six sturdy twigs cut to equal lengths and tied together with jute twine make an easy but stylish star. Hang it under a window frame and up-light it with a candle to create an atmospheric corner. A few lengths of ivy also make a natural, festive finishing touch, wrapped around the base of candles or tied to banisters. If possible, display them in the coldest rooms in your house so they last for as long as possible.

HEAD GARDENER'S JOB
❧ OF THE MONTH ❧

Apple tree pruning at Downhill Demesne, County Derry
Head Gardener – Una Quinn

The National Trust looks after many orchards, spanning 50 miles of Northern Ireland's headland. At Downhill Demesne, the orchard is part of the Walled Garden, which originally produced fresh food for the flamboyant 'Earl Bishop' household from 1784 to the 1940s.

Pruning has many benefits for our apple trees. We remove dead, damaged and diseased branches this month to strengthen the trees and help prevent or slow the spread of pests and diseases. Pruning also stimulates strong growth of new fruit-bearing branches, and improves light-access and air circulation, which encourages a strong fruit harvest. We also prune our apples to help develop and maintain balanced trees that are an even shape. With damaged and diseased material, we always prune back to healthy growth. We make swift, clean cuts, using loppers for smaller stems and a pruning saw or a bow saw to remove larger branches. Sharp, clean tools are essential because open wounds on a tree are a gateway to the pathogens of disease.

Nearby to Demesne, the whitewashed and thatched Hezlett House (1691) is home to an orchard that provides a bumper crop to a beloved community apple-press event each October. Orchards are a great joy that provide multi-sensory thrills: apple blossom, birdsong and buzzing wildlife, while in December, blackbirds scavenge forgotten fruits.

❧ PLANTS OF THE MONTH ❧

Sarcococca confusa
This is a superb choice for a shady place that gets walked past frequently in winter. For most of the year, it's a fairly unremarkable evergreen shrub but in winter its hanging, spidery white flowers give off the most delicious scent. You'll come up with any excuse to go outside and walk past. It grows best in moist, well-drained soils that don't dry out quickly. Height: 1.5m (5ft).

Euphorbia 'Silver Swan'
This sun-loving, drought-tolerant perennial gets its name from the neat silver edges of its light green leaves, which add valuable structure to the garden and patio this month, giving it a frosted look. In spring it shows off gently cascading white bracts with red 'eyes'. Grow it in a

D

sheltered corner or near a house wall to prevent the leaves from being damaged by cold weather and grow in free-draining soil or compost. Height: 1m (40in).

Pinus heldreichii 'Smidtii'

If you've been put off by the thought of conifers after seeing ones that look like skyscrapers, try this pint-sized plant, to add evergreen texture to the garden through winter. It is very slow growing, unlikely to exceed 30cm x 30cm (12in x 12in) in 10 years. Great for patios, rockeries or even troughs, it is best grown in full sun in soil or compost that drains well. Height: 30cm (12in).

❧ WILDLIFE TO LOOK FOR ❧

Bank vole

Rather than hibernating, this tiny, chestnut-brown mammal stays active all year round. In December, you could possibly see one darting around looking for scraps that have fallen from a bird feeder. They have cream-coloured bellies and a short, hairy tail. They are rapid movers, so you have to be sharp to spot one. They tend to create burrows in grassy areas and feed mainly on fruit and nuts as well as small insects.

Deer

As food becomes more difficult to come by, deer can leave their mark on gardens this month by eating bark from trees. They usually feed at night and are gone before dawn, leaving something of a phantom presence in the garden. Inserting stakes around the trunk of the tree can stop deer getting close enough, or you can wrap tree guards around the base.

Violet ground beetle
This shiny beetle
is very much a
gardener's friend,
feeding on slugs
and snails. They
are likely to be
at rest during
the day in log
piles or compost
heaps before coming
out at night to hunt.

Violet ground beetles are flightless but can scurry away
quickly when they have to.

❧ HOW TO HELP WILDLIFE ❧

If you have a pond, make a point of checking each morning
to see if it has frozen over. If the pond freezes, toxic gasses can
build up and kill fish and amphibians that are in the water.
Floating a football in the middle of the pond will help prevent
it from freezing over. If your pond has frozen, place a hot (but
not boiling) saucepan of water on the surface of the ice to
gently melt it. Breaking the ice by force can cause harm to fish.

❧ BIRD OF THE MONTH ❧

Robin
They may feature on many Christmas cards, but December
can be a tough time for robins if the ground is frozen
or covered in snow. Robins find food by searching the
ground for insects, which is why they can so frequently

D

be seen hopping around lawns and veg patches. It's also why they may start following you when you are gardening, in the hope that if you disturb soil, you'll unearth a tasty gem or two for them. If you've got a bird table, they will be particularly happy to see mealworms and fat balls.

❧ GARDEN EVENTS ❦

World Soil Day, 5 December
A UN-led campaign to help highlight the importance and environmental benefits of healthy soil and the role it plays in society.

Tree Dressing Day, 7–8 December
A practice celebrated all over the world, tree dressing helps highlight the important role that trees play in our lives. Look out for opportunities to get involved in your local community, with schools encouraged to take part.

Christmas Events
Many National Trust properties are a sight to behold this month, bedecked in their festive finery with many special events taking place too. Soak up the sights, sounds, smells and flavours of the season at the Garden of Lights event at Blickling Hall, Norfolk, or experience the decorated rooms at A Winter's Night inside Gunby Hall, Lincolnshire.

Festival of Winter Walks
The Ramblers festival has been running (or should that be walking) for more than 25 years. Look out for a group walk near you or go on your own walk, exploring the library of Ramblers Routes.

NATIONAL TRUST GARDENS
❧ AT THEIR BEST ❧
(for Christmas lights and winter illuminations)

Anglesey Abbey, Cambridgeshire

Look forward to the Winter Lights spectacular, which each year has a theme, and has partnered with local authors and illustrators to put on a show to remember.

Trivia

A Sequoia sempervirens (coastal redwood) in the Dell at Bodnant Garden appears in the Guinness Book of World Records as the tallest in Britain at 45m (148ft).

Kingston Lacy, Dorset

Christmas Lights at Kingston Lacy include the after-dark trail through the illuminated garden, where you will be entertained by a series of light installations. Look out for tunnels of light and glistening trees.

Belton, Lincolnshire

Discover a staggering one million-plus twinkling lights and seasonal sounds filling the air with the festivities of the season. Wander beneath glistening trees lit with dramatic colours and walk through illuminated tunnels.

Trengwainton, Cornwall

Take a stroll through the walled garden under the warm glow of strings of fairy lights. Enjoy illuminated structures along the way, created by local schools and artists, and hang a bauble on the wishing tree.

D

Gibside, Northumberland

The after-dark illuminated trail includes giant baubles, larger-than-life illuminations and dramatic flickering flames, encouraging you to pause and reflect as you spend time in the fire garden.

Trivia
The first house bought by the National Trust was Alfriston Clergy House in East Sussex. It was bought for the sum of £10 in 1896. It was saved from being demolished and is still owned by the Trust and open to visitors.

'At no time in the cycle of seasons do you get that feeling of "here we go again" so strongly as in winter.'
– Christopher Lloyd

YOUR NOTES FOR
❧ NEXT YEAR ❦

What has worked

_____
_____
_____
_____
_____
_____

What hasn't

_____
_____
_____
_____
_____
_____

What I'd like to try

_____
_____
_____
_____
_____
_____
_____

D

Index

Many thanks to Storm Dunlop for compiling the sunrise and sunset pages.

Weather data supplied by the Met Office
© Crown copyright 2023, the Met Office